This is a photocopiable resource.

Boost Creative Writing Confidence at KS2 by Kate Long

Index

Introduction and Warm-up Exercises..p 5-13

Part One

1. Beginnings (story-writing)..p 17
2. Openings (story-writing)..p 19
3. Where's the Best Place for a Story to Begin? (story-writing)...p 21
4. Creating Characters out of Names Part 1 (story-writing).........p 23
5. Creating Characters out of Names Part 2 (story-writing).........p 25
6. Creating Characters out of Names Part 3 (story-writing).........p 27
7. Planning a Long Story: the 3X3 Method (story-writing)............p 30
8. Fantasy Room (description)..p 33
9. Inside the Castle (story-writing)..p 35
10. Superheroes (character)...p 37
11. Villains (character)..p 40
12. Hamster Fun (story-writing)..p 43
13. Two Flies (playscript)...p 45
14. Dreams (poetry)..p 47
15. To Someone Special (poetry)...p 49
16. The Colour of Happiness (poetry).......................................p 52
17. Hidden Messages (poetry)...p 54
18. Endlings 1 (story-writing)..p 56
19. Endings 2 (story-writing)...p 59
20. Endlings 3 (story-writing)..p 61

Part 2

21. Lost Belongings (character)...p 64
22. Appearance (description)..p 66
23. Guess What's Wrong With Me (character)............................p 69
24. Tragic Ted (story-writing)..p 72
25. Face Mats (character)...p 74
26. Disappearing Whales (poetry)..p 78

Boost Creative Writing Confidence at KS2 by Kate Long

27. On Another Planet (description)...p 81
28. The Magic Ring (story-writing)...p 83
29. Spoon Wars (playscript)..p 85
30. Shells (poetry)..p 87
31. Werewolves! (persuasive writing)..p 90
32. Horror Scopes (non-fiction writing)..p 94
33. Lifetime Achievement Award (non-fiction writing).......................p 99
34. Tiny, Rubbish Superpowers (non-fiction writing)........................p 102
35. Gotcha! (playscript)...p 104
36. A Rap (poetry)...p 105
37. Line Breaks (poetry)..p 107
38. Mushrooms (poetry)..p 111
39. Crows (editing)..p 113
40. Dandelions (poetry)...p 117

Part 3

41. Precious Jewels (poetry)..p 121
42. I Am (personal writing)..p 124
43. Bubbles (poetry)..p 126
44. Peacock Feathers (poetry)...p 129
45. Snails (poetry)...p 133
46. Gothic Tales (story-writing)..p 137
47. The Invasion (story-writing)...p 140
48. The Magic Door (poetry)..p 143
49. Woodlice (poetry)..p 148
50. Conkers (poetry)..p 151

Boost Creative Writing Confidence at KS2 by Kate Long

Boost Creative Writing Confidence at KS2 by Kate Long

Shh — a Trade Secret!

There are many times as a writer that the blank page inspires only dismay. Where to begin? How to get off the starting blocks? Your heart sinks. You freeze. Your head empties of creative thought. You cannot think of a single thing you want to say. And this is just as true for adult professional authors as it is for children in the classroom. How *do* you make the words come? Where on earth are they, and how do you reach them?

Well, there is a simple trick, an exercise, a method of training your brain that helps draw those words out so they flow freely onto the page in a way that's relatively painless and often surprising.

Some authors refer to it as "flash fiction", others call it "morning words", but the process is essentially the same. It's about silencing your inner critic, silencing your conscious, controlling writer's mind, and letting the subconscious take over. In practical terms that means choosing a prompt word or picture or idea, setting a timer for 2-5 minutes, putting your pen to the paper, and simply writing. You write fast. You don't stop to read back what you've written; the time for editing is afterwards. You write whatever comes into your head, splurging it down on paper, not worrying about how good it is or whether it makes much sense. If you find you're stuck, then you write your last word over and over until the next sentence pops into your brain. It's even OK to write "I can't think of anything" as a holding phrase until the next set of ideas come. The main thing is to keep your pen moving, and to stay inside that bubble of concentration until the time is up.

If children in the classroom are trained to do this before they start a creative writing session, it genuinely makes a difference to their confidence and engagement. The brain is warmed up using an exercise which no one else is going to read and which can go straight into the bin afterwards. No one's going to mark it or ask them to correct any SPAG. It's served its purpose by freeing up the creative cogs and getting the students 'into the zone'.

Boost Creative Writing Confidence at KS2 by Kate Long

It might take a while to acclimatise the children to working this way; some will be resistant, especially children who tend to be perfectionists and want everything to be right first draft. Others will be tempted to glance over at their friends' work to see how that's coming along, or prematurely try to share something they've written themselves. So it's important to stress the need for complete individual focus and silence, and the need to keep writing *without pause*. And if some children write very very slowly and only manage half a sentence, that doesn't matter as long as they write.

It's worth adding that sometimes the results turn out to be surprisingly good, and students want to read their work out straight away, or keep it and continue at home. But if that happens, it's a bonus. This is about the process, not the product. Really, the purpose is to switch on the writing-brain, ready for business.

Warm-up Exercises

Boost Creative Writing Confidence at KS2 by Kate Long

Why Warming-Up is Crucial

Warming up for a creative writing session is as important as warming up before an exercise class.

Although a few children will happily take to this idea of 'just covering the paper with writing', most will need a week or two before they're ready to let go. So for the first couple of sessions, make the warm-up a fast-as-you-can dictation exercise where you call out a word and they write that over and over till you change it for another. Keep the dictation words very simple so no one has to pause to ask for a spelling. At the end of a minute their page might read "egg egg egg egg man man man bat bat bat bat bat bat bat hand hand frog frog book". The idea is to get the students used to their pen moving quickly and without too much deliberate thought behind it.

Once they feel confident about writing freely and without pausing, you can move onto other warm-up exercises.

This kind of training also encourages the brain to produce creative ideas under time-pressure, which can be an extremely productive way of working. The guided writing activities and many of the poetry activities in this book call on that ability.

One of the hardest things to do as a writer is to turn off the self-censor, but if you can do it, the writing flows so much more easily!

Boost Creative Writing Confidence at KS2 by Kate Long

First Line Prompts

Ask the children to copy down a short but dramatic opening phrase or sentence from the board. They then have three, four or five minutes to carry the story on. Stress you are not worried about spelling or punctuation, and that they won't have to read out what they've written. It's just about writing fast, and seeing what comes out.

Some opening prompts I've used:

The door creaked open.

"Help!" cried Alex.

The spaceship had landed.

We were lost.

Under the sea…

Thunder rumbled.

Someone was watching me.

Inside the cave…

I know a secret.

The hamster had escaped!

Sometimes the results of this exercise can be impressive, and children should be encouraged to keep and carry on any good beginnings at a later date.

Word Association

Tell the students they are going to hear and write down a word, (word 1), and then they have to write underneath it the first word that pops into their heads (word 2). Then underneath that, write the first word they associate with word 2. Then underneath that, the first word they associate with word 3, and so on till they have made a long list down the page. Do an example list on the board before you start, talking through your own thought processes as you scribble.

It might go:
bird (opening prompt word)
egg
nest
tree
volcano (I don't know why; that's just what came into my brain!)
fire
screaming
wasp
yellow
banana
custard
wellies (Again, I'm not sure where this came from.)
beetle
ladybird

Opening prompt words I've used include 'danger', 'jungle', 'red', 'king', 'ice', 'shadow' and 'midnight'. Sometimes a child instead of the teacher provides the prompt word for the group.

Afterwards students love to talk about how they got from the first to the last word on their list, and any unusual leaps they made along the way. It can be a bit dull to hear everyone's list being read out, but it's fun to go around the class and listen to everyone's final word, given that they all began with the same prompt.

Some children have very logical links, while others will be much more off-beat and lateral. That's because we are all individuals and all have our unique writing voice.

Boost Creative Writing Confidence at KS2 by Kate Long

Word Webs

Photocopy the web graphic on the next page, or get the children to draw their own on blank paper. Give a prompt word for them to write in the centre, and see how many words related to that single, original word the children can think of in three or four minutes.

For example, using the prompt word "silver" you might get:

gold

sparkle   coins

moonlight   precious

silver

tinsel   treasure

fish   bracelet

spoon

Boost Creative Writing Confidence at KS2 by Kate Long

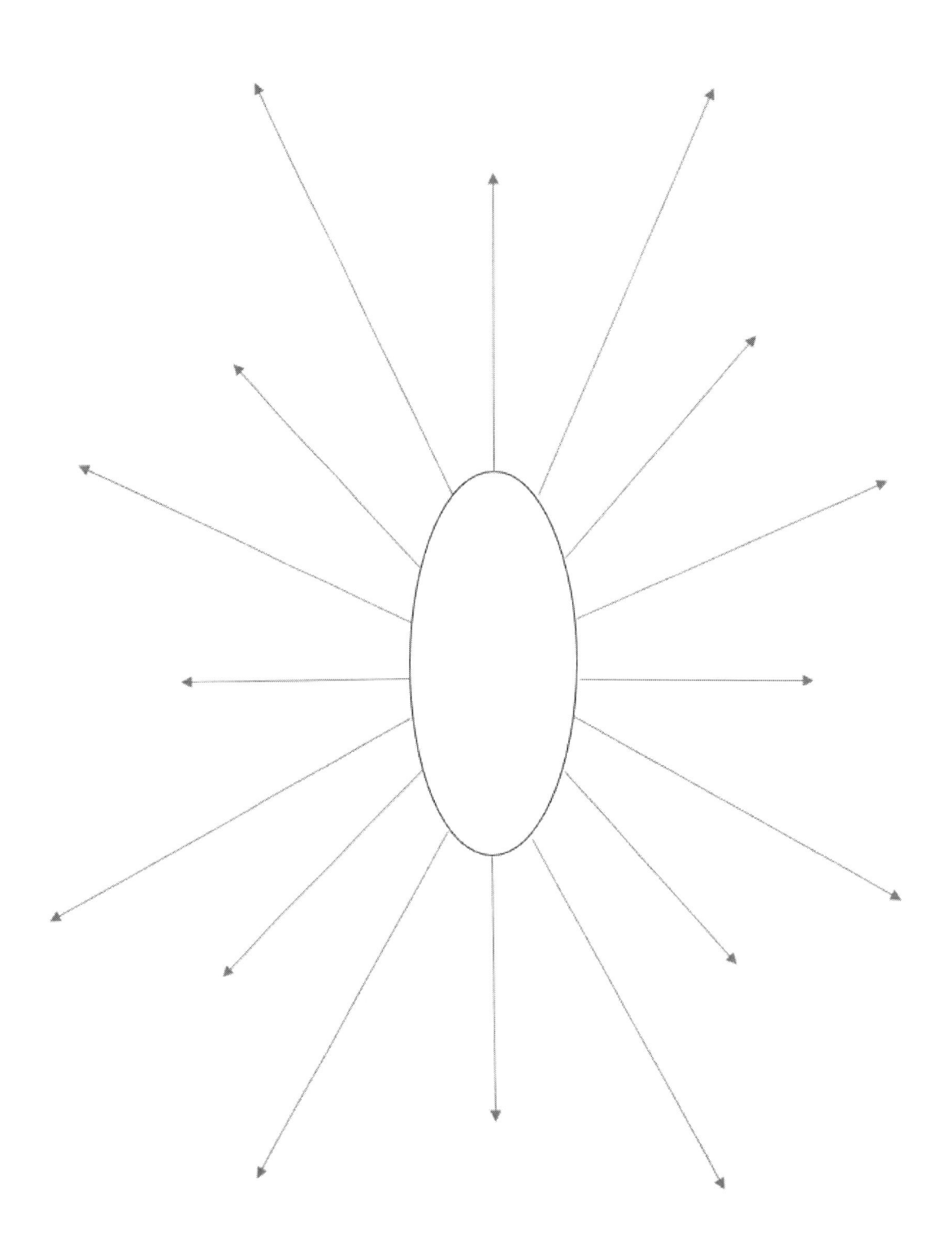

Boost Creative Writing Confidence at KS2 by Kate Long

Uses For

This can be done in groups or pairs or as well as an individual exercise.

Show the children an ordinary household or school object such as a pair of socks, a beanbag, the lid off a jam jar, a paper clip.

Tell them they have to list as many uses for the object as they can, and they need to be super-creative in their ideas. For example, you could use the socks:

- as sleeping-bags for a couple of mice.

- to stuff up the nostrils of a dragon and stop it breathing out fire.

- to block out the noise of the speakers when you're on stage playing lead guitar at a rock concert, etc.

Maybe at the end the children could vote for who came up with the best suggestion.

How this book is organised

In deference to the busy lives of teachers, I've divided the exercises into three sections.

The first, and largest, come under "easy preparation" — at most you'll need to photocopy a sheet or two in advance of the lesson.

The second group need "some prep" — you might need to take in an everyday item as a prop, or go online and print off an image, or bookmark a YouTube clip.

The third (smallest) group I've categorised as "frankly a bit of a faff", in that you need props which you might not immediately have to hand. But what I will say is, the results are worth it. These lessons have gone down incredibly well with the students and produced some stunning work. So they'd make a nice once-a-term event if you're after something special.

Writing Activities 1

(easy prep)

Boost Creative Writing Confidence at KS2 by Kate Long

1. Beginnings (story-writing)

Preparation: Photocopy a set of the Some Opening Lines worksheet.

1. Warm-up exercise.

2. Discussion in groups or pairs:

- Why are story beginnings so important?

    Give out the list of first lines and ask the students to read them, then put them in rank order, starting with their favourite.
    Discuss as a class. Which are the most popular? Which are the least?

    Why?

    What are lines 3, 4 and 6 trying to do? *(Raise questions that the reader wants answering.)* What's 8 doing? *(Establishing sci fi genre.)* 2? *(Establishing setting.)* 1? *(Establishing a not-serious tone.)* 5? *(Establishing a dramatic tone.)*

- So what jobs might an author have to do within the first few lines? *(Establish the setting/main character or narrator/genre/tone/pace.)*

3. Now ask the students to write a terrible opening line to a story. It can be any genre, but it must be really rubbish.

    Share and laugh. Offer back-to-front praise ("No, sorry, that's too good!").

4. Now ask the students to write a great opening sentence. Remember, not all stories have to start with a bang.

5. Share. Try to establish what each student's first line is trying to do – is it creating a mood, getting straight into the action, setting the genre or introducing a key character?

6. If there's time, let them carry on and complete a whole first paragraph.

Boost Creative Writing Confidence at KS2 by Kate Long

Some Opening Lines

1. Mrs Crab was a nasty, mad old woman with staring eyes and hair that looked like someone had dropped a pile of dirty twigs on her head.

2. Wind lashed at the stunted trees, and ragged clouds raced across the moon as Tom struggled home.

3. All her life Emma had only wanted one thing.

4. 'Whatever is that noise?' said Mr Fitton, sticking his face out of the bedroom window in alarm.

5. Joe knew almost immediately he was in trouble.

6. It wasn't my idea.

7. Most cats are just cats.

8. Mira had never seen a spaceship as huge as the Star Cutter.

Boost Creative Writing Confidence at KS2 by Kate Long

2. Openings (story-writing)

Preparation: make photocopies of The Start of the Trouble worksheet on the next page.

1. Warm-up exercise.

2. Discuss: why is it so important that, as story-writers, we get our opening paragraphs right? Is there anything that would put you off in an opening paragraph?

3. Give out the sheets and read through the three openings together. Then ask the children to read through them again on their own and annotate any words or lines they thought were good, and any they didn't think were as successful. Finally they should rate the openings, first-second-third.

4. Discussion again: what's the story basically about? What genre do you think it might be? How much do we learn about the main character?

   Ask what notes the children have made on a), then b), then c).

   What's it called when we explain the background to a character's life? *(Backstory.)* And it's always tricky to know how to feed that in when really you want to get on with the action. Which opening deals with backstory the best? Which was the most effective opening, and why? Which one did you like the least?

5. Now the children can write their own openings about a teenager setting off on holiday and disaster striking.

Boost Creative Writing Confidence at KS2 by Kate Long

The Start of the Trouble

a) The first sign something was wrong was when the stewardess came out of the cockpit, frowning. I saw her check her watch, then tap her colleague on the shoulder. The two women whispered together, a look of growing alarm on both their faces. In the seat next to me, Mum flicked the screen of her iPad; she hadn't noticed the strange, new, tense atmosphere. But now I glanced around the plane, I could see other passengers had picked up on it too. My heart began to beat hard.

b) We were two hours into our flight when something went wrong. Oh, by the way, my name's Chris and I'm 17 and I live in London with my mum Shelley. We were going on holiday to Miami because a distant relative had died that summer and left us some money. My mum works really hard as a doctor; she said she needed a long, sunny break to recharge her batteries. When she mentioned America, I thought my dreams had come true! I just knew that trip was going to be the best ever. But how wrong I was.

c) "Haven't you packed yet?"

Mum's annoyed voice travelled up the stairs to where I sat in my room, surrounded by a sea of clothes, games, chargers, tubes of hair gel and sun cream. What should I pack for a fortnight in Miami? It would be hot, I knew that; I'd been checking the temperatures every day. Not like grey old London, with its washout summer.

Boost Creative Writing Confidence at KS2 by Kate Long

3. Where's the Best Place for a Story to Begin? (story-writing)

Preparation: Make photocopies of the Sequence of Events worksheet.

1. Warm-up exercise.

2. Discuss: where do you start a story? How do you find the beginning? Do top fiction books generally begin, '**One day I woke up and decided to have breakfast. I got dressed and then went downstairs. Because it was Sunday, I decided to make porridge, and so I poured some oats into a bowl and added milk. Then I stirred the mixture round and put it in the microwave for two minutes. It was delicious. Afterwards I washed up and poured myself some orange juice. Then I went next door and watched cartoons on TV for an hour.**'

   No, because this is dull and you need to get on with some action.

3. Give out the Sequence of Events worksheet and read it through together. This is the plan for the first half of an adventure story. But where would be the best place for the story to start? (Give the children a moment to write an asterisk against the number where they think the story should begin.)

   Discuss: do we need 1? Do we need 2? Can 2 be fed into the story as background? ('**Jude ran, panting, across the precinct. All day she'd been hiding from Alisha's gang, dodging through the corridors, peering round corners, hiding in the toilets at lunchtime. But now they'd caught up with her, spotted her as she tried to slink quickly through the school gates, and that was it, the pursuit was on.**')

   Can we start the story as late as 4?

4. Ask the children to write the first part of the story, or more if there's time.

5. Share and give feedback. Does anyone have an idea how the story might end?

Boost Creative Writing Confidence at KS2 by Kate Long

A Sequence of Events

1. Jude gets up and goes to school.

2. Jude has a bad day being bullied.

3. After school, Jude is chased by a gang of bullies into a rough area of town.

4. Jude hides in an empty garage.

5. While hiding, Jude witnesses some criminals arguing.

6. There's a vicious fight and one of the criminals is badly, perhaps fatally, injured.

7. What next?

Boost Creative Writing Confidence at KS2 by Kate Long

4. Creating Characters out of Names, Part 1 (character development)

Preparation: make photocopies of the character names sheet on the next page.

1. Warm-up exercise.

2. Discussion: what's in a name? Do the children like their own names? Do they ever wish they were called something else? Can you tell what someone's going to be like just from hearing their name? Say two or three random names and see what kind of images are conjured up in the children's heads, but choose names of people not in school so there's no obvious association.

3. Give out the sheet of character names (Bomber, Mrs Butterworth etc) and ask the children to pick one from the list, whichever they fancy, and draw a ring around it. Then give them a minute to focus and picture that character. When everyone's ready, go round the group hearing ideas. Try to pin down the basics every time: is your character male or female? How old? General colouring? General body shape?

4. If at the end any names haven't been chosen, you might want to talk about what you yourself imagine for that character. Point out how sometimes names suggest someone's background, e.g. Major Pennington.

5. Now ask the children to jot down notes on what their character looks like, using as much detail as they can, especially when it comes to hair and clothing. How is their hair styled? Do they spend a lot time on it, or none at all? Are their clothes branded? In good or bad condition? What's on their feet? Footwear often says a great deal.

6. Tell the children, "Your character is carrying a bag. Describe the bag, then write down at least three things that are in there."

7. Share! There will probably be lots to discuss, not least where the children think their ideas came from. But if you still have time left in the session, go onto Part 2.

Boost Creative Writing Confidence at KS2 by Kate Long

Character names

Bomber

Mrs Butterworth   Angel

Albert Dawes   Saleem

Major Pennington   Cora

Sammy Stone

Ziggi   Marta Peplinksi

Boost Creative Writing Confidence at KS2 by Kate Long

5. Creating Characters out of Names, Part 2 (character development)

Preparation: make photocopies of the Character Questions sheet on the next page.

1. Warm-up exercise.

2. Ask the children to remind themselves of the character they created, then draw her/him. At least 10 minutes spent sketching and labelling that character is a useful investment of time here because it will enable them to get back into that world they created. Tell them they can add more information as they draw, if they want to.

3. Give out the list of questions and read through them together. Ask the students to pick one, focus on that and see if they can answer it in as much detail as possible. A single sentence response is fine, but a short paragraph is better. When they finish that question, tell them do another, and then another. Give the class a good 15-20 minutes on this exercise, so that by the end they should all have answered at least three questions. If any of them race through and say they've finished, they can either go back to their drawing, or think of three more questions (and answers) for their character.

4. While they're working, you might like to write a list of character types on the board to help with discussion later. These could include: **leader, bossy, laid-back, sporty, troublemaker, sneak, friend-splitter, loner, bully, big-head, dreamer, crazy, kind, aggressive, loyal, adventurous.** Or anything you like!

5. Share and discuss at length. Some children will be amazed by how much they have discovered about their character, and how real she/he seems.

This is a technique used by lots of professional fiction writers and it's sometimes called 'hot-seating'. I used it myself to generate material at the start of every novel I planned.

Boost Creative Writing Confidence at KS2 by Kate Long

Some Questions for your Character

What's the worst physical injury your character's ever suffered?

What's the most disappointing Christmas present your character's ever received?

What's the most disgusting thing your character's ever eaten?

What does your character keep in the bottom of the wardrobe? And on the top?

Does your character have a phobia? How did it start?

Has your character ever shoplifted or stolen anything? Why?

What's your character's biggest secret?

Boost Creative Writing Confidence at KS2 by Kate Long

6. Creating Characters out of Names, Part 3 (story-writing)

Preparation: make photocopies of the opening Break-in! story on the next page. Maybe print out a dramatic image from *Macbeth* to illustrate your story as you read it?

1. 1. Warm-up exercise.

2. Put the children into pairs, then ask them to give their partner a brief summary of the character they created. At the end of the description, their partner should ask for another bit of random information about that character's life, so the hot-seating continues. This is important to help the students get back into the world they created. If anyone's stuck for something new to ask, try: what's his/her job, where does she/he like to go on holiday, who's his/her best friend, who's her/his worst enemy. Stop when everyone's had a turn at being the questioner.

3. Discuss: character IS plot. If your character is in a plane crash, do they stop to help others or do they just run away and save themselves? If your character finds a lost purse full of money, what do they do with it? (Remember, your character is not YOU. We know you would return the purse.) If your character takes the money, what do they use it for?

   So your characters often decide the way in which the story's going. Always listen to your characters!

4. Tell the story of Macbeth: **Mediaeval Scotland, and two Scottish lords, Macbeth and his friend Banquo, are riding across a moor at night. Suddenly they stumble across three spooky witches who reveal to Macbeth that one day he will become king. It's a completely unexpected prophecy! He hurries home and tells his wife, who is as excited by the news as he is. Neither Macbeth nor Lady Macbeth can see how it can happen, but they really want the prophecy to come true. They are both madly ambitious people.**

Boost Creative Writing Confidence at KS2 by Kate Long

The next week the king himself comes to stay at Macbeth's castle. Remember, Macbeth is DESPERATE for the prophecy to become real. What might he do to help the prophecy along?
(See if you can prompt the children into saying "murder him".)

The witches also told Macbeth that although he'd become king, he wouldn't get to keep the throne. It would pass to the son of his friend Banquo. Macbeth hates that idea. What does he decide to do? *(Sets out to murder his friend and his friend's son.)*

How would the story have been different if Macbeth had been a nice man, or a loyal or patient one?

5. As writers, you need to test your character to find out who they really are. Put them into dramatic situations and see how they'll behave. Imagine: your character is in bed, asleep, at night, when they wake suddenly. There are strange noises coming from downstairs. It's pitch dark and the sounds are getting louder. How does your character react? What action do they take? Carry on the Break-in! story and see what happens…

Break-in!

_____ woke with a terrible shock. It was two o'clock in the morning, and someone was creeping about downstairs.

Boost Creative Writing Confidence at KS2 by Kate Long

7. Planning a Long Story: the 3X3 Method

Preparation: make copies of the ***beginning middle end*** sheet on the next page.

1. Warm-up exercise.

2. Discuss: ask the children if they've ever imagined life as an animal, not a human? Lots of stories feature people being changed into animals – 'The Witches' by Roald Dahl (a boy turns into a mouse), many Greek myths e.g. the hundred-eyed guardsman Argos being turned into a peacock, 'The Silver Chair' by C S Lewis (a prince turning into a serpent), 'Jennie' by Paul Gallico (a boy turns into a cat), 'Dogsbody' by Diana Wynne Jones (a man turns into a dog).

3. Read the opening to Franz Kafka's 'Metamorphosis'.

   One morning, when Gregor Samson woke up, he discovered that he had changed into a giant beetle. He lay on his beetle back and saw, as he lifted his head, a brown, arched stomach divided up into ridged sections. The blanket was sliding off his beetle body, and his thin little legs waved about helplessly in front of his eyes.

   Reactions? Is this a good opening to a story? Would they read on?

4. Ask the children what they think is going to happen to Gregor Samson. Will the story turn out happily or badly?

5. Show them the 'beginning, middle, end' sheet and read it through together. Stress this is not how the real story ends, but it's one way things could have turned out for Gregor Samson.

6. *Talk about the advantages of splitting a story plan up into beginning, middle and end, and then splitting each part into three again. Why might it be useful for a writer to see exactly where a story's headed? (So you can see how much there is to go; so you can see how much time to spend on each section; to make you feel more confident about the direction of your story.)*

7. Ask the students to pick an animal, then imagine they wake up like Gregor Samson and find they've magically turned into that animal. How would they feel? What would their families think?

   - Can they now sketch out a plan showing a beginning, a middle and an end to their story? If they've managed that, can they look at splitting a section into three and adding more detail, like the sheet does? How much detail are they able to add?

8. Sharing ideas.

Obviously if the children are keen, they can carry on and write the story, either one section of it or the whole thing.

beginning

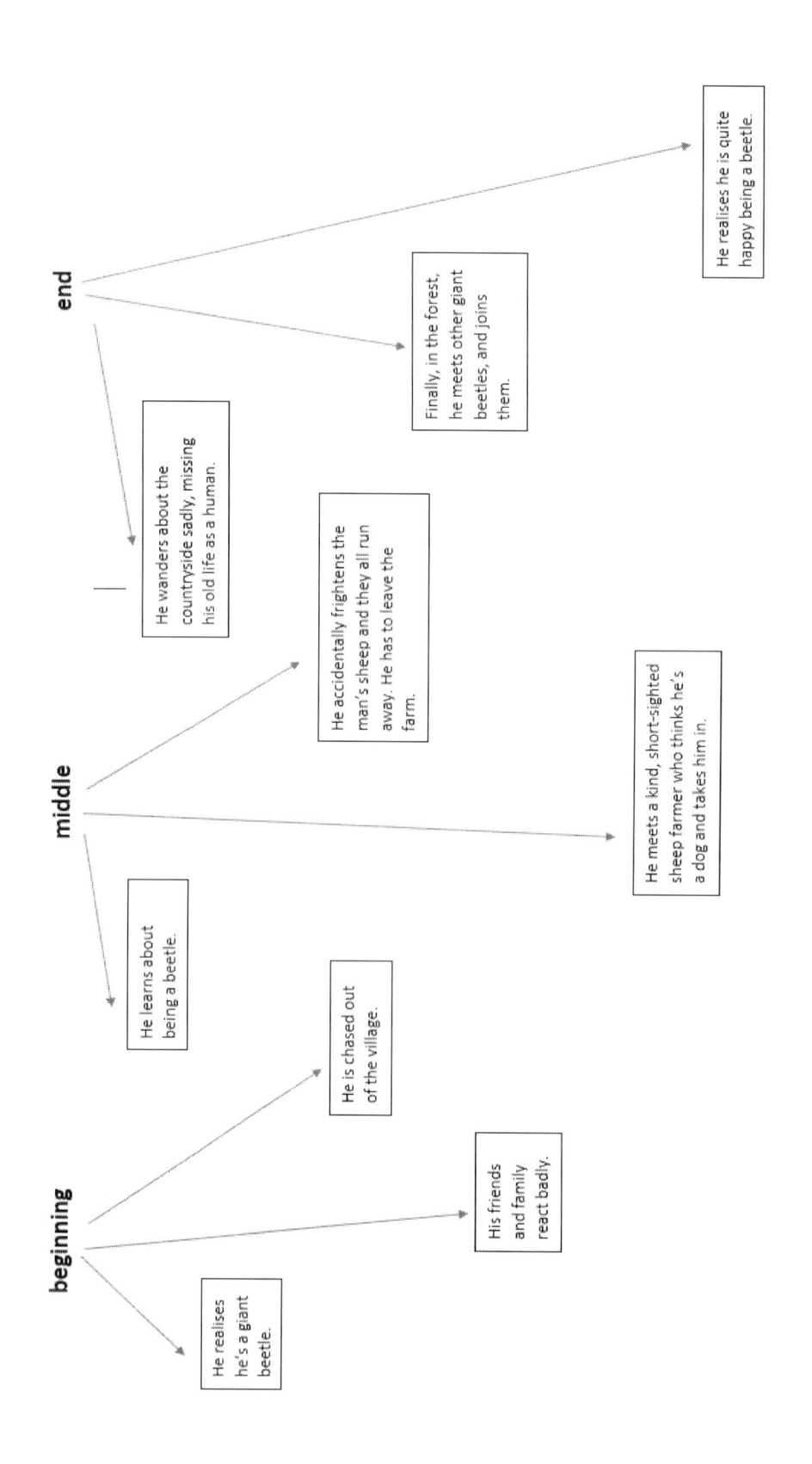

- He realises he's a giant beetle.
- His friends and family react badly.
- He is chased out of the village.

middle

- He learns about being a beetle.
- He meets a kind, short-sighted sheep farmer who thinks he's a dog and takes him in.
- He accidentally frightens the man's sheep and they all run away. He has to leave the farm.

end

- He wanders about the countryside sadly, missing his old life as a human.
- Finally, in the forest, he meets other giant beetles, and joins them.
- He realises he is quite happy being a beetle.

Boost Creative Writing Confidence at KS2 by Kate Long

8. Fantasy Room (description)

Preparation: none, unless you want to gather a pile of fantasy books from the school library to help the discussion.

1. Make your warm-up prompt something to do with monsters.

2. Discussion: what is fantasy writing? Can anyone name a fantasy film or book? (*The Hobbit*, the *Narnia* books, *Harry Potter* series, *Charlie and the Chocolate Factory* and most of Roald Dahl's books, *Alice in Wonderland*, *A Series of Unfortunate Events*, the *Percy Jackson* books, *Inkheart*, the *Redwall* series, *Mary Poppins*, the *Marvel* superheroes, *How to Train Your Dragon*, the *Beast Quest* series…) Which ones are your favourites? So how would you define "fantasy" as a genre?

3. Tell the children they are going to do some guided fantasy writing. Read out these prompts at whatever pace suits the group – some of these will need plenty of space. If anyone gets stuck, dictate the bracketed line to start them off, or tell them to miss that detail out and wait for the next one. Remind the students to write in complete sentences.

   - **Take a moment to picture an amazing door. What shape is it? What's it made of? What colour? It has an unusual knocker: what's that like? OK, now write a sentence describing that door.**

   - **You open the door. What's the first thing you see? (You could start, "When I opened the door…")**

   - **How big is the room? It's full of — what? (You could say, "The room was…")**

   - **You walk forward. What's the floor like? What's it made of? ("Under my feet…")**

- There's a mirror on the wall and you catch sight of your face — how do you look? (Suddenly, across the room I spotted…")

- A staircase lies in front of you. Describe it. Is it spiral? Wide? Steep? Rickety? Dark? ("In front of me…")

- You start climbing the staircase and a smell drifts down towards you. What is it? How does it make you feel? ("Climbing the staircase…")

- At the top of the staircase is a painting that chills you to the bone. What's it of? ("I stopped at the top to look at…")

- You walk into the first room you come to. In the centre of the room is an old wooden chest. Describe it. ("The first room…")

- You lift the heavy lid and inside is a pile of stunning treasure. Pick three items and say what they are. ("When I lifted the lid…")

- You decide to steal one of the items, but as you lift it out, you hear a noise. What is it? ("I decided I would take…")

- A hideous face appears in the doorway. It's the monster who guards the treasure! Describe the creature who's about to pounce on you. ("To my horror I noticed…")

- In panic, you rush to the window and climb out onto the sill. What can you see below you? ("I dashed for the window…")

- Meanwhile the monster crosses the room swiftly. With a thudding heart you turn away, launch yourself and jump… In your final sentence, say what happened next. ("The monster charged…")

If anyone's working very fast and waiting for others to catch up, ask them to go back and add detail to what they've already written.

4. Share and give feedback.

5. If there is any time left, the children could draw an illustration to go with the story.

Boost Creative Writing Confidence at KS2 by Kate Long

9. Inside the Castle (story-writing)

Preparation: none.

1. Warm-up could be 'the key'.

Tell the children this story: **You've been invited by a distant relative to stay at an ancient castle in France. The castle sits on the side of a mountain, overlooking a black lake, and surrounded by forest. It's a lonely spot. You're not sure you're going to enjoy staying there for a week because there's no Wi-Fi, the electricity keeps going off and the nearest shops are too far away to walk to. The relative you're staying with is very old and doesn't much like talking, and there's no one else to chat to except the miserable cook and the nervous gardener. So in a fit of boredom, you go exploring.**

The castle is a large, cold, grey, rambling structure with narrow windows and stone walls. There are four sets of winding staircases leading up into turrets, though you've been told not to climb them as they lead to the roof and the roof is strictly out of bounds and dangerous.

As you pass through the entrance hall, however, something bright green catches your eye. It's a parrot, perching on a wooden rafter. How has it got there? As you watch, it takes off and flies out of the room, down one of the gloomy corridors in a flash of startling colour.

How can you not follow? You run after the bird, your feet pounding along the stone tiles. It swoops in front of you, teasing, then glides away into the distance. You're enjoying the chase. This is the most exciting thing that's happened this week. But when you round the corner, the parrot's gone. Disappointment floods through you. Where can the it be? Wait — is that a green feather on the bottom step there? You dart forward, and yes. A sharp tail feather, like a spear. You pick it up, admiring the way the light gleams exotically along its length. Then from somewhere above you, you hear wings fluttering. The parrot must be further up the stairs. Gripping the feather in one hand, you start to climb.

You know you shouldn't be going up into the turret. But you have to find that parrot. It might need rescuing. It might hurt itself, or it might be hungry or thirsty. Why has your relative never mentioned it? Maybe it's a wild bird

Boost Creative Writing Confidence at KS2 by Kate Long

that's got in by accident. Do they have wild parrots in France? Your thoughts whirl in your head as you go higher and higher.

And then you're at the top and there's just a window in front of you. The parrot is sitting on a rafter above your head, as if waiting. When you reach up to stroke it, it hops away, out of your reach. It looks as if it's laughing at you, this parrot.

Disappointed, you turn your attention to the window instead. It's filthy, covered in grime so you can't see the view. You take your sleeve and rub it against the glass, but that only smears the dirt around; instead you unlatch the window and open it wide. The parrot makes a happy squawk — and at the same time, something tinkles onto the stone floor. What is it?

With a screech, the parrot swoops down and rushes for the window, past your head. Shocked, you cover your face against the flapping wings. When you open your eyes, the parrot has flown right through the window and is sailing off over the treetops towards the dark lake. But now you can see what it as that dropped onto the floor; what it was that made the tinkling sound. At your feet is weighty, ancient key that looks as if it opens somewhere important. The parrot has left you a present.

2. Discussion: what might this key be for? Has the main character's holiday been very exciting so far? *(No. So we need something to happen that is exciting.)* How much freedom does the main character have? *(Lots! There are no responsible adults about.)* Whereabouts in the castle is dangerous? *(The roof, the black lake, perhaps the forest.)* What other hazards might you find in an old castle? *(Crumbling steps, wells, oubliettes/dungeons...)*

3. Individually, or working in pairs, the children should carry on the story so that the main character uses the key to have an adventure.

4. Sharing and feedback.

10. Superheroes (character)

Preparation: make photocopies of the list of superhero questions on the next two pages.

1. Warm-up exercise.

2. Ask the children to make a list of super-heroes. They can be from books comics, films or TV. You could start them off with Wonder Woman, just to make the point that superheroes can be male or female.

3. Discussion: who's on the list? What kind of things do superheroes get up to? Why do we like stories about superhumans?

4. Tell the children they are going to come up with their own superhero. Give out the sheets for them to fill in.

5. Sharing and feedback.

6. As a follow-up in another session, they could use those characters to write their own superhero stories.

Super Powers!

-What's your super-character called?

-Is he/she on the side of good or evil?

-What's his/her motto or battle-cry?

-What does his/her badge look like? What's his/her costume?

-What special gadgets or equipment does he/she use?

- What vehicle does he/she use to get around, and what special features does it have?

-Where is he/she based? What does his/her lair look like?

- How did he/she acquire their super-power in the first place?

-What is his/her main weakness?

Boost Creative Writing Confidence at KS2 by Kate Long

-Who is his/her sidekick?

-Who is his/her arch-enemy?

-What is the greatest moment of his/her career?

-Does he/she have a disguise like Superman does, where they blend into everyday society? If so, what's the day job?

- Make a quick sketch of your super-character here.

11. Villains (creating characters)

Preparation: make photocopies of the Questions for Villains sheet on the next page.

1. Warm-up exercise.

2. Start telling the story of 'Megamind': **two alien babies with superpowers fall mysteriously to earth. One lands in a prison yard and is found and brought up by tough male convicts; the other lands near a young married couple and is brought up in a warm, happy and financially secure family unit. The prison-raised child struggles at school and is bullied, which makes him retaliate which means he's bullied and hated more. Meanwhile, the child who ended up with an adoring mum and dad does well at school and is popular with his peers and teachers, and makes terrific progress. As time goes on, the prison-raised child becomes bitter at his miserable life and decides to take matters into his own hands by toughening up and fighting back. He mainly shuns friendship, which he assumes is weakness, and does whatever he wants. He grows up to be a selfish, power-obsessed super-villain, reviled and feared by all. The other boy, blessed at every step, becomes a superhero and gains fans and accolades everywhere he goes.**

   Ask if the children know the film? What happens after that? *(If you don't know the film yourself, the villain eventually finds love and friendship and turns his life around and becomes a hero.)*

3. Villains in fiction – how many can the children name? Make a list on the board together. It could include:

Snape, The Dursleys, Voldemort, the Malfoys etc (*Harry Potter*)

The Grinch

Scrooge

Miss Hannigan (*Annie*)

Cruella de Vil (*101 Dalmations*)

Sid Philips (*Toy Story*)

Boost Creative Writing Confidence at KS2 by Kate Long

Aunt Spiker and Aunt Sponge (*James and the Giant Peach*)

Miss Trunchbull (*Matilda*)

Kronos (*Percy Jackson*)

The White Witch (*Narnia*)

The Joker (*Batman*)

Darth Vader (*Star Wars*)

Mr Burns (*The Simpsons*)

Hans (*Frozen*)

The Daleks, Missy (*Doctor Who*)

General Woundwort (*Watership Down*)

The Child Catcher (*Chitty Chitty Bang Bang*)

Count Olaf (*Lemony Snicket*)

Mrs Coulter *(His Dark Materials)*

Julian *(Wonder)*

4. Ask: why are baddies important? *What* do they do for a story? *(They provide plot movement, create tension and conflict, arouse the readers' emotions, create a contrast and a challenge for the hero.)* Choose a specific villain and talk it through. **What does he/she do, plot-wise? What's his/her motivation? What's his/her darkest deed? What made him/her so evil? Do you at any point in the narrative have a glimmer of sympathy for this villain? Is that a good thing for the story?**

5. Give out the sheets and tell the children they are going to create their own villains.

6. Sharing and feedback.

7. The next stage would be to write a scene where the villain is terrorising someone. That scene could then be developed into a whole story.

Boost Creative Writing Confidence at KS2 by Kate Long

Create your own villain.

You will need to explain:

a) what sort of childhood he/she had.

b) if anything happened to them in their teenage or young adult years that really knocked them back - what mistakes they made which led them further down the path of villainy. For instance, did they hook up with someone nasty? Did they become fixated on some humiliation or injustice which they should have just walked away from?

c) what's their chief motivation? (Revenge? Power? The creation of general mayhem/destruction? The retrieval of something lost?)

d) what might redeem them (if there is anything – they could just be a lost cause!)

e) if there are any limits on the type of evil they do – are there acts which are simply too evil even for them?

f) what's the worst thing they've ever done?

Create your own villain.

You will need to explain:

a) what sort of childhood he/she had.

b) if anything happened to them in their teenage or young adult years that really knocked them back - what mistakes they made which led them further down the path of villainy. For instance, did they hook up with someone nasty? Did they become fixated on some humiliation or injustice which they should have just walked away from?

c) what's their chief motivation? (Revenge? Power? The creation of general mayhem? Getting back something they lost?)

d) what might redeem them (if there is anything – they could just be a lost cause!)

e) if there are any limits on the type of evil they do – are there acts which are simply too evil even for them?

f) what's the worst thing they've ever done?

Boost Creative Writing Confidence at KS2 by Kate Long

12. Hamster Fun (story-writing)

Preparation: none required for the immediate activity, but my group wrote up their stories into mini books. So you could assemble some materials for them to do this – a long-armed stapler, for instance, and some pre-cut pages – and also provide a few images of hamsters for them to copy if they want to illustrate the story. It might even be nice to watch a video of funny hamsters before you start.

1. Warm-up exercise.

2. Read out this opening:

The bedside clock said midnight but Maggie couldn't sleep. She was too excited.

Over in the corner of the room sat a brand new hamster cage, and inside it, a brand new hamster. She'd gone with her mum earlier that day to choose him: a coffee-coloured ball of fluff with a pink nose and neat white paws. 'I'm going to call him Podge,' Maggie had said as the shopkeeper scooped him out of the tank and popped him into a little cardboard box. She was shaking with excitement as they drove home.

And all day she'd been waiting for him to come out and play.

'Leave him be for a few hours,' her mum had urged. 'He'll be frightened. He'll need time to get used to his new home.'

So Maggie had sat impatiently, unable to concentrate on anything else because she kept glancing over at the cage and hoping Podge would show.

Now, at last, it sounded as if the hamster might be awake. She sat bolt upright and began to push back the duvet eagerly.

'Hey!' came a piping voice from the corner. 'You! Come over here.'

Maggie stared. By the faint light coming through from the landing she could see that Podge had indeed come out. More than that, he was standing up on his hind legs and stretching a stern, skinny paw through the cage, as if to beckon her.

'Yes, you,' repeated the hamster. 'Big human. Come here. I've got something important to tell you.'

Boost Creative Writing Confidence at KS2 by Kate Long

3. Discuss the story so far.
    -What kind of personality does this hamster have? Is it mischievous, domineering, sneaky, plain evil?
    - How will Maggie react? Will she be scared, delighted, stunned?
    - What does the hamster have to say to her?
    - Is she going to share this news with anyone, or keep it a secret?
    - What kind of adventures could you have if you owned a talking pet?

4. Discuss possible scenarios that could develop from this opening such as taking the hamster to school, using it to spy on people or to burgle houses, entering it for a talent show.

    Some of the children might want to use a different talking animal for their story, especially if they haven't much experience of hamsters.

5. Let the children write, then share their stories. Even if they haven't got very far they can still explain how the plot is going to unfold.

Boost Creative Writing Confidence at KS2 by Kate Long

13. Two Flies (playscript)

Preparation: photocopy the Two Flies playscript opening on the next page. Have an example of a simple playscript ready to show on the projector in case anyone's not sure of how to set one out.

1. Warm-up exercise

2. Make sure everyone knows how to set out a playscript. Go through an example if necessary.

3. Give out the Two Flies script and read it through together. Reactions? What sort of a fly is Nippy? What kind of a personality does Buzz have? How might the world look differently to a fly? What do you think is going to happen — happy or sad ending to this tale?

4. Tell the children they are going to carry on the Two Flies script. They should try and bring the story to a close by the end of the session, so you'll give them a ten-minute warning. For an exercise like this, they could work individually or in pairs.

5. When time's up, hear the stories and give feedback.

Boost Creative Writing Confidence at KS2 by Kate Long

Two Flies in the Kitchen

*A filthy kitchen with towering piles of plates, half-eaten food, cat biscuits scattered on the floor and a dish of mouldy fruit on the windowsill. Two flies, **Buzz** and **Nippy**, are stalking up and down the worktops, assessing the situation.*

Buzz: I don't know, I've been in worse places.

Nippy: But we're trapped!

Buzz: Yeah. I get that. Until someone goes out through the back door or opens a window, we're stuck. Still, I don't think we'll starve, do you?

[Buzz flies over to what was once a plate of baked beans and paddles about in the juice happily.]

Nippy: Well, I don't like it. I'm the sort of fly who needs freedom. I'm a wild creature. I'm not a pet. I want to be outdoors in the sunshine.

Buzz: It's raining.

Nippy: Not the point.

Buzz: If you'd got shut in next door's kitchen you'd have something to complain about. That lot keep their house so clean it's disgusting. Every surface shines, there's nothing to eat... It's as if they didn't care about helping flies at all.

Nippy: And I've heard they use [whispers] fly spray.

Buzz: Eugh! Don't even speak about such things! They're murderers, that's what they are.

[Nippy joins Buzz in the bean juice.]

Nippy: But what if we never get out? I can't bear the thought of it. Trapped in here forever. Left to die behind the cooker. The tragedy! - Oh, hang on, who's this coming now?

Boost Creative Writing Confidence at KS2 by Kate Long

14. Dreams (poetry)

Preparation: make photocopies of the Dreams sheet on the next page.

1. Warm-up exercise.

2. Discussion: what are dreams? What do you think causes them? What's the weirdest thing you've ever dreamed? How can dreams make you feel?

   Tell the class about Mary Shelley dreaming up the plot of *Frankenstein*. Dreams can sometimes give us creative ideas to work with.

   What are daydreams? How are they different from the dreams you have when you're asleep? Are they useful, harmful, or just fun?

1. Give out the Dreams sheet and talk about the first three examples. What kind of dreams are these? *(Longings, hopes, ambitions.)*

   Try a few as a group. What do you think a dog dreams of? What do you think a Christmas tree dreams of? An iceberg?

   Give the children as long as they need to fill in the sheet. As usual, tell them that if they get stuck, just leave it move onto the next one. Not every line has to be completed, and some of their lines will be better than others.

2. Share. The children could choose their 6 - 10 best lines and then copy them up for a display, perhaps along the lines of the dream jars in The BFG. There are plenty of jar templates available online, and glitter pens and stick-on jewels would make the jars look magical.

Boost Creative Writing Confidence at KS2 by Kate Long

Dreaming, Dreaming

An icicle dreams winter will never end.

A fossil dreams of restless, prehistoric seas.

A raindrop dreams of thundering waterfalls.

What do these objects dream of?

An owl

A bare tree

A candle

A cloud

A nest

A star

An acorn

A feather

A river

A sheep

A dandelion

A woodlouse

A desert

A cobweb

A lost glove

An unborn baby

Boost Creative Writing Confidence at KS2 by Kate Long

15. To Someone Special (poetry)

Preparation: none. However, if the children choose a family member to write about, this poem makes a lovely Christmas activity because they can copy the poem out neatly, roll it up, tie the scroll with ribbon and give it as a present. So plain paper, guidelines and paper clips, felt tips/crayons/gel pens/glitter pens and a bit of gift ribbon will be required for the next part.

1. The warm-up activity might be something to do with 'love'.

2. A quick game: ask the class, if _____ were an animal *(name a confident child who will enjoy the attention)*, what sort of animal would she/he be? Listen to suggestions. In each case, ask why. Then, if _____ were a type of sweet, what would she/he be? And if _____ were a type of weather?

3. Tell the children they're going to write a poem about someone important in their lives. It can be a parent or grandparent, a sibling, some other family member or just a very dear friend. Let them take a moment to think about that person, and why he or she means so much. In the poem, every line is going to compare that person to something pleasant or positive. But you are also trying to capture the essence of that person; what it is that makes them so special.

So I might say: My son is a busy squirrel
A slice of tangy lime
The scent of deep pine forest
A comet streaking across the sky
etc.

Boost Creative Writing Confidence at KS2 by Kate Long

4. Ask the children to write the name of the person at the top of the page, then the opening line (choose whichever one is appropriate): "**My Mum/Dad/Grandma/brother/aunty/friend is...**" Then start the prompts. Remind them that if they get stuck on one, just to leave it blank and wait for the next.

   - **Something that's brightly coloured**
   - **Something that's particularly nice to touch**
   - **Some type of beautiful light** *(stars, sunset/sunrise, light on water, fireworks, flames, birthday candles)*
   - **Some kind of exciting treat**
   - **Something delicious to eat**
   - **An animal you really like**
   - **A lovely sound**
   - **A nice fragrance or smell**
   - **A time of day that you always enjoy**
   - **A place that makes you happy or safe**
   - **One positive word that sums that person up** *(or just repeat the person's name)*.

5. If these poems are quite personal, the children might not want to share, but they will enjoy writing them up and decorating them. And honestly, the recipients of the poems will be thrilled.

Boost Creative Writing Confidence at KS2 by Kate Long

Here is a class poem written to celebrate the birth of a teacher's new baby:

A new baby is

A bright buttercup in summer

The soft fur of a kitten

A newly-planted tree

An undiscovered flower

A candle to brighten your life

Christmas morning every morning

A brand-new colour you've never seen before

A present to be unwrapped

A silk blanket

The soft touch of a rose petal

A bright star from another galaxy

A freshly-picked strawberry

The tune of a wind-chime on a dawn breeze

The giddy rush of sky-diving

A new-spun spider web sparkling in the dew

Sunlight reflecting off a lake

The beginning of the world.

Boost Creative Writing Confidence at KS2 by Kate Long

16. The Colour of Happiness (poetry)

Preparation: make photocopies of the Emotions sheet.

1. The warm-up exercise might be 'If I won the lottery...'

2. Discussion: what makes you happy? I mean madly happy, thrilled, beside yourself? Think of some things. What was the happiest you ever were in your life? What did that make you feel like physically? (The children can jot down ideas.)

3. What makes you frightened? – Ditto. List physical symptoms.

4. Angry? Sad?

5. Share ideas. Tell the children they're going to try and describe those emotions. But why is it harder to describe rage than, say, a dog or a shoe? *(Because rage is abstract and the other things are concrete, you can see them and pick them up and handle them.)* So what writers do when they try to describe abstract things is to reach for comparisons, similes and metaphors. These are extremely useful tools for a writer.

6. Give out the Emotions sheet on the next page. Read the poem at the bottom of the page. Reactions? Do they recognise any of those sensations?

7. Ask the children to choose a feeling to focus on (they can use the list at the top of the page, or come up with their own) and try to remember a specific occasion when they felt that way. Then using the list of prompt questions, they should write their own.

8. Sharing and feedback.

Emotions

anger   sadness   loneliness   fear

happiness   relief   love   courage   hope

1. A colour
2. A taste
3. A smell
4. Something you'd find in Nature
5. An item of clothing
6. A physical sensation
7. What it makes you want to do

Boredom is a foggy grey

It tastes of stale water

Smells of damp

It is a gloomy forest stretching towards the horizon

In every direction

Boredom lies across my shoulders like a soaking wet scarf

*   weighing me*

*   down*

It's an ache under my ribcage

It makes me want to tear at the wallpaper with my fingernails.

Boost Creative Writing Confidence at KS2 by Kate Long

17. Hidden Messages (poetry)

Preparation: make photocopies of the poem on the next page.

1. Warm-up exercise.

2. Give out the poem. Let the children read through it and ask for reactions. Then tell them there's a hidden message: can they spot it? *(It's an acrostic poem where the first letter of each line spells out I KILLED YOUR GOLDFISH.)*

3. Tell the children they are going to write their own poems containing hidden messages. They can be apparently nice poems with a sting in the tail, or just messages you might be too shy or nervous to tell someone. But the secret message should be spelt out using the initial letters of each line, like the example they just read. Possible subjects: you've done something wrong but you're too scared to confess; you want to reveal how you truly feel about someone; you're setting a clue to help someone solve a puzzle, e.g. where you've buried treasure.

4. When the children have finished, get them to read their poems out very slowly, emphasising the first word of each line. The rest of the class can try to crack the code!

Boost Creative Writing Confidence at KS2 by Kate Long

Welcome Back Off Your Holiday, Dear Neighbours

It's wonderful to have you home! I've cleaned your

Kitchen and hoovered your hall,

I've got fresh milk in and a loaf of bread —

Look in the fridge! I got you bacon too so you can have

Lovely bacon sarnies for breakfast tomorrow morning.

Every room is spotless because I went round and

Dusted, and I even cleaned your windows.

You're such great neighbours, it's a pleasure to help.

On Tuesday the paperboy came and I paid your bill —

Usually he comes on Saturday I know but he'd been ill —

Really, don't bother to pay me back. It was only a tenner.

Go upstairs and you'll see I mended your curtains; they

Only needed stitching at the bottom where the hem had come loose.

Luckily I had some thread the exact shade of blue! Well, I

Didn't really, but I went and got some from the shop. No bother.

Friday, I mowed your lawn and painted your garden bench.

It looks smashing now, I think you'd agree. I've just been longing

So, so much, my dear neighbours, to have you

Home.

Boost Creative Writing Confidence at KS2 by Kate Long

18. Endings 1 (story-writing)

Preparation: make photocopies of the Endings worksheets on the next page.

1. Warm-up exercise.

2. Discuss: Endings - are they easy to write, or tricky? Can anyone think of an example of a good ending in a film or book? Any examples of bad endings? Does an ending have to be happy? What does an ending have to do? *(Resolve things – assure you that the characters you've been following have a future. Also, wrap up loose ends.)* What do you think of cliff-hanger endings, where we're not sure what happened next? *(You could mention 'The Italian Job'. The children won't have seen it, but you could describe how the robbers end up teetering on the edge of a cliff and that's how the film closes.)*

3. Talk about the main types of ending, and ask for examples and if the children like them.

    - surprise/twist ending, e.g. 'The Paper Bag Princess', 'Adolphus Tips'.
    - mixed happy/sad ending, e.g. 'Mary Poppins', 'The Witches'.
    - moral ending, where the baddies get punished and the goodies are triumphant, e.g. 'Matilda', 'Granny'.

4. Explain that if you get stuck about how to end a story, try the technique of writing down as many reasonable possibilities as you can. Give out the Sam sheet on the next page and ask the children to see if they can come up with three possible endings for this plot.

5. Discuss. If there's time, they could do the second sheet too.

6. Finally, tell the children they need to ask themselves what they want their ending to say about life. Is it fair or unfair? Do they want to give their reader a warning about something? Do they have a message? *(Criminals always get caught. Loyalty pays. Stand up to bullies.)* Think of some endings where there is a message — 'Wonder', 'Despicable Me', 'Frozen', '101 Dalmations'.

Boost Creative Writing Confidence at KS2 by Kate Long

Endings Worksheet 1

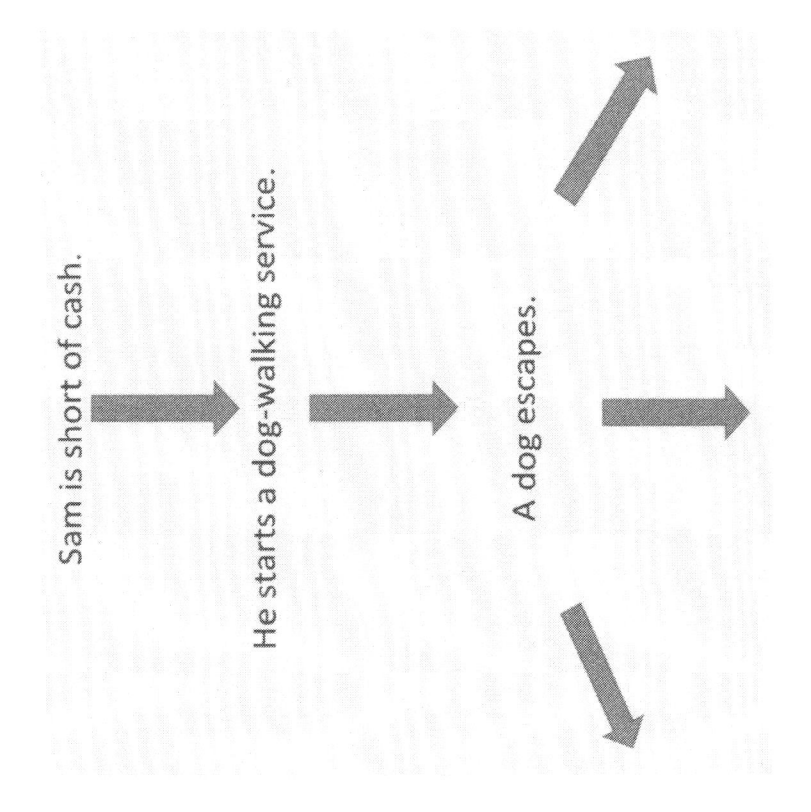

Sam is short of cash. → He starts a dog-walking service. → A dog escapes. →

Boost Creative Writing Confidence at KS2 by Kate Long

Endings Worksheet 2

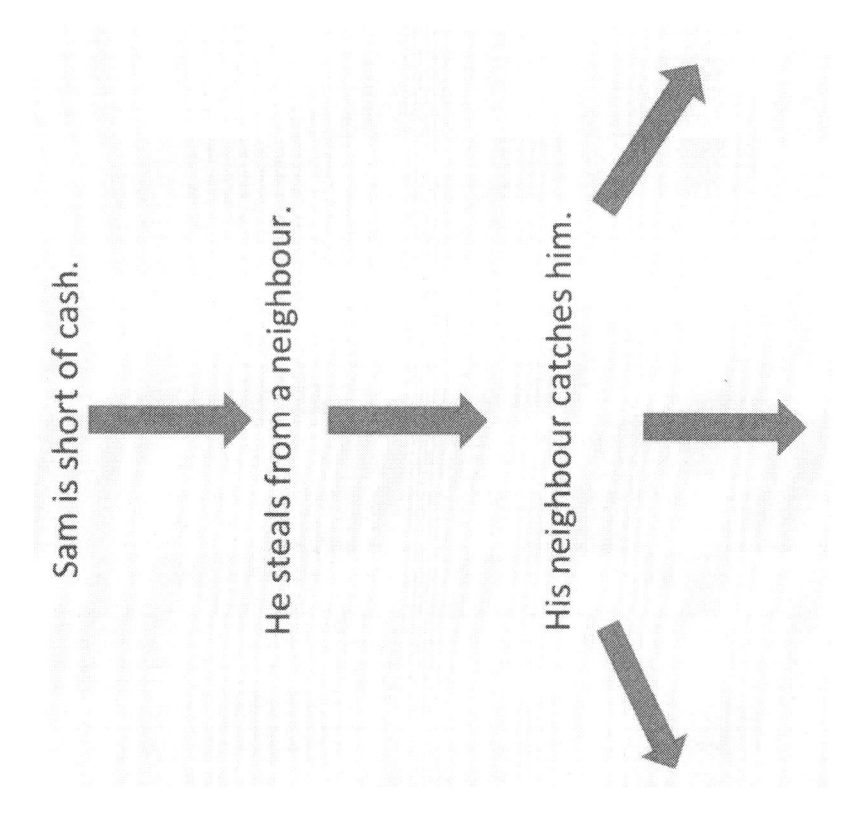

Sam is short of cash. → He steals from a neighbour. → His neighbour catches him. →

Boost Creative Writing Confidence at KS2 by Kate Long

19. Endings 2 (story-writing)

Preparation: make copies of the *Ruthin, Wales* sheet on the next page.

1. Warm-up exercise.

2. Give out the sheet and read through the beginning of this story together. Reactions? Whose side are the children on? Will it be a happy ending for Tommy, or not?

3. Let the children continue the story. Stress you're really looking for them to get an ending on.

4. Share and give feedback.

Boost Creative Writing Confidence at KS2 by Kate Long

The year: 1890. The place: Ruthin, Wales.

Panting hard, Tommy scrabbled at the factory gate. He could hear the steps of the policeman coming up fast behind him, but he didn't dare look round. His heart was hammering so loudly now, the blood in his ears sounded like crashing waves. His ribs heaved as he tried to catch his breath.

"Stop right there, son!" came the shout.

Tommy's fingers tugged in vain at the metal bolt. It was too heavy for his small hands to shift. He glanced up, trying to work out whether he could somehow jump or climb the gate, but it was taller than he was and topped with vicious metal spikes.

Suddenly a tight grip was on the back of his collar, wrenching and twisting the cloth so that for a few seconds he almost choked.

"Now, my lad, I've got you! You're not going anywhere – except to prison, once the magistrate's had a look at you." The policeman shook him like a dog.

"It wasn't me," gasped Tommy. "It was another boy."

"Then why were you running?"

"I – I just ran. I dunno."

"Just ran?"

"Yeah."

"And just happened to have a pocket stuffed full of cash?"

With his free hand, the policeman pointed grimly to the cobblestones at their feet. They were littered with coins, glinting shillings and florins and half crowns, that had fallen out of Tommy's coat as he twisted and squirmed.

"It's… it's my brother's, sir. It's his wages. He asked me to collect them for him."

The policeman sneered.

"Do you expect me to believe that?"

"I dunno, sir. Yes, sir."

Carry on the conversation between Tommy and the policeman. Who has Tommy stolen the cash from? Why does he need money so badly? Does the policeman have any sympathy with the boy, or is Tommy off to jail?

Boost Creative Writing Confidence at KS2 by Kate Long

20. Endings 3

Preparation: make copies of the Gareth sheet on the next page.

1. Warm-up exercise.

2. Give out the sheet and read through the beginning of this story together. Reactions? Do they have sympathy with Gareth? What kind of a life is he currently leading? What might be waiting for him in the woods?

3. Let the children continue the story. Stress you're really looking for them to get an ending on.

4. Share and give feedback.

Gareth

Gareth was going home late again because someone had hidden his rugby boots and he'd had to stay behind to look for them. Finally he'd found them in a bin by the school entrance. The work of Kyle Morris, he bet. That's who usually took his stuff. That's who, last term, had thrown his PE bag so high up a tree that no one could reach it and his mum had to buy new. Fourteen weeks' pocket money, it had cost him. His dad had been furious. "Just tell us who did it," he'd urged. Gareth had shaken his head. So then it was like he'd thrown the bag away himself. "Why don't you stand up for yourself?" his dad had snapped. *You try standing up to someone literally twice your size*, he wanted to reply.

Now it was getting on for 5 o' clock and dropping dark, and when he got home he'd be in trouble again. That's why he took the short cut through the woods.

Gareth

Gareth was going home late again because someone had hidden his rugby boots and he'd had to stay behind to look for them. Finally he'd found them in a bin by the school entrance. The work of Kyle Morris, he bet. That's who usually took his stuff. That's who, last term, had thrown his PE bag so high up a tree that no one could reach it and his mum had to buy new. Fourteen weeks' pocket money, it had cost him. His dad had been furious. "Just tell us who did it," he'd urged. Gareth had shaken his head. So then it was like he'd thrown the bag away himself. "Why don't you stand up for yourself?" his dad had snapped. *You try standing up to someone literally twice your size*, he wanted to reply.

Now it was getting on for 5 o' clock and dropping dark, and when he got home he'd be in trouble again. That's why he took the short cut through the woods.

Writing Activities 2 –

(small amount of prep)

Boost Creative Writing Confidence at KS2 by Kate Long

21. Lost Belongings (creating characters)

Preparation: assemble a random bunch of costume jewellery, preferably including men's items like cufflinks and tie pins, and some unisex items like badges. If you can't get hold of any, print out some pictures.

You can also do this with scarves, or shoes, or purses/wallets, or bags, or gloves—any small, personal items. If you're using pictures instead of the actual items, then you can go bigger — coats, cars, even houses.

(An additional spin on this is to use one single prompt for the whole class — a carrier bag— and fill it with a range of items which you bring out one after another, giving the children time to deduce the kind of owner and refine that deduction every time a new object appears. You can spin a bit of a yarn about where the bag was found, if you like.)

Make photocopies of the Character Questions sheet.

1. Warm-up exercise.
2. Give out the pieces of jewellery, or whatever you're using as prompts. Let the children have a really good look at what they've been given, then close their eyes and imagine the person it belongs to. When they have an idea of the person's sex and age, they should open their eyes and jot that down, along with any other basic details they've thought of at this stage, e.g. a **name, height and body-shape, colouring, hair type**.

3. Ask them to draw a quick sketch of that person, including any details of clothing they can conjure up. If they get stuck, refer them back to the prompt object and get them to look for clues (is the item expensive or cheap? Flashy or modest? In mint condition or shabby? Fashionable or outdated? Does it include any logos or motifs that might indicate a hobby or interest?)

4. Give out the character question sheet and ask them to fill in as much as they can.

5. Share. The children can then use this character to write a story.

Character Questions

When your character looks out of the bedroom window each morning, what does he/she see?

Your character's on a train and there's a horrible, badly-behaved, noisy child in the opposite seat. How does your character deal with the situation?

What does your character smell of?

Who is your character's favourite person in the world? Who is their second-favourite?

Your character has a fierce ambition: what is it?

Which TV personality winds your character up, and why?

What pet(s) does/did your character have? Why choose this animal?

What was your character's proudest moment in life?

Boost Creative Writing Confidence at KS2 by Kate Long

22. Appearance (description)

Preparation: print/cut out a selection of photographs of not-famous people. Try to cover a wide range of ages, ethnicities, styles and facial expressions.

Make photocopies of the Character Descriptions sheet on the next page.

1. Warm-up exercise.

2. Discuss: do you, as readers, like to know how a character looks? What does Gangsta Granny look like? Greg Heffley from *Diary of a Wimpy Kid*? Alex Rider? Why is it important to you?

3. Give out the Character Descriptions sheet and ask the students to assess both pieces of writing as if they were teachers. Tell them to tick anything that's good, and write comments in the margin. Ask which passage is better, and why? At the end of the passage B, why doesn't it say, "I thought she was cool"? *(Because there's no need. It's implied throughout.)*

    Explain that, in description, DETAIL is what counts. For realism, use specific brands, colours, styles, and don't forget to mention imperfections.

4. Spread the photos out on the tables and ask the students to choose one. Tell them they are going to write a detailed description of that person as if they were seeing him/her for the first time.

    You could write these prompts up on the board to help start them off:
    - **What is their hair like?**
    - **What are their eyes like?**
    - **Is there anything unusual about them, e.g. a scar, facial hair, ear rings, piercings?**
    - **What's their general expression?**
    - **How are they dressed (not including shoes)?**
    - **What's on their feet?**
    - **How do you imagine they walk?**
    - **How do they make you feel as you look at them?**

Boost Creative Writing Confidence at KS2 by Kate Long

5. Share and get feedback. An extension of this exercise is to put the character into a scene where they approach and speak to you – maybe they approach you in the street and ask you to help find something they've lost.

Copyright-free images below, but you'll probably want to choose your own.

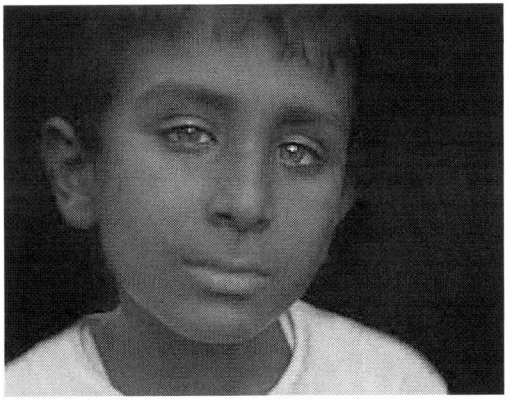

Boost Creative Writing Confidence at KS2 by Kate Long

Character Descriptions

A. The girl was pretty but her clothes were shabby. She walked along the pavement. I thought she was cool.

B. The girl's hair was a sheet of gold in the sunshine, flowing carelessly over her shoulders and down the back of her denim jacket. Her eyes were wide and ice-blue with long, dark lashes. She walked like she owned the world. As she drew closer, though, I saw the hem of her skirt was frayed and splashed with mud, and her Converse trainers looked about ready to fall apart. The cuffs of her lace shirt were grubby. She spotted me staring; stared right back. You could just tell nothing ever scared her.

Character Descriptions

A. The girl was pretty but her clothes were shabby. She walked along the pavement. I thought she was cool.

B. The girl's hair was a sheet of gold in the sunshine, flowing carelessly over her shoulders and down the back of her denim jacket. Her eyes were wide and ice-blue with long, dark lashes. She walked like she owned the world. As she drew closer, though, I saw the hem of her skirt was frayed and splashed with mud, and her Converse trainers looked about ready to fall apart. The cuffs of her lace shirt were grubby. She spotted me staring; stared right back. You could just tell nothing ever scared her.

Boost Creative Writing Confidence at KS2 by Kate Long

23. Guess What's Wrong With Me (character)

Preparation: write out some personality types on slips of paper and fold them up or put them into envelopes. If you like, for extra drama, you can write them on rice paper with edible pen so the children can keep their assigned personality secret by eating it!

1. Warm-up exercise.

2. Writers don't always spell out everything – read the children this short passage and ask them to listen to how Ally's feeling.

   "I'm going to be late for school again," said Ally, looking at her watch for what felt like the hundredth time.

   At the kitchen table, her little sister Beth swung her legs and smirked. She was actually eating her cornflakes one by one, Ally noticed. Anything to drag out breakfast for as long as possible. Every morning was the same. Unbelievable.

   "Dad! Dad? Can you not hurry Beth up?" she called.

   But he was on his phone, talking about some work thing.

   Ally gripped the strap of her school bag tightly and tried not to think about the science test first lesson.

   How can we tell what's going on here? List on the board all the emotions Ally's feeling. Why do writers sometimes use clues and leave us to guess? *(Because it's more interesting for the reader; because it draws you into the story.)*

3. Give out envelopes. In each one, there's a character trait (type) – you're going to read it, memorise it, then destroy it.

Then you're going to write a scene featuring a character who shows this trait very strongly, and when you've finished, you're going to read yours out and we'll try and guess what your character trait is.

4. First, decide whether your character is going to be male or female. Give them a name. They are adults, but how old are they?

5. Now choose one of these situations *(write these up on the board)*:
    - Your character's best friend wants to borrow some money off him/her.
    - Your character has got his/her head stuck between some railings.
    - Your character asks his/her next door neighbour to help with a job, e.g. digging a pond, putting up a tent, baking cakes for a summer fair.
    - Your character has gone for a job interview.
    Describe how it went!

6. Read and guess!

Some possible character traits

vain	**spiteful**	**aggressive**
competitive	**immature**	**nervous**
jealous	**boastful**	**arrogant**
lazy	**silly**	**mean**
selfish	**bossy**	**greedy**
grumpy	**rude (not polite)**	**unkind**
untidy	**lying**	**cheeky**

Boost Creative Writing Confidence at KS2 by Kate Long

24. Tragic Ted (story-writing)

Preparation: get hold of a battered teddy bear (I got mine from a charity shop) and batter it a bit more. I daubed mine with paint, removed an ear, tore its fur near the leg and undid some of the stitching on its nose.

Don't be squeamish about this; it's in a good cause.

1. Warm-up exercise could be 'lost'.

2. Discussion: who has a favourite teddy? Tell us about it and some of the adventures it's had. How much do these childhood toys matter?

3. Bring out Tragic Ted. Point out the bear's defects. Explain to the children, they're going to recount the story of how this teddy got its injuries.

4. Deliver prompt questions, to be answered in complete sentences/paragraphs. As usual, go at whatever pace the children need, and tell them that if they can't think of an answer to a question, just leave it and wait for the next one.

Boost Creative Writing Confidence at KS2 by Kate Long

- What is the teddy's name?
- Who was its first owner? What was he/she like?
- What kind of life did the bear have there?
- While in this house, the teddy lost an ear. How did that happen?

- Another time, the teddy got dropped somewhere outside and left behind for three days. It was then the teddy's nose got damaged. What happened?
- Another time, the teddy was attacked by an animal and that's when the leg got ripped. What happened?
- Another day, the teddy was taken to school. That's where the blue paint happened. Tell the story of how that came about.
- What will happen to the teddy now?

5. Share ideas and give feedback.

25. Face Mats (character)

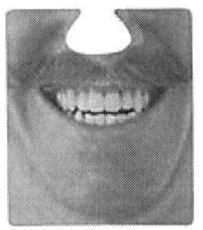

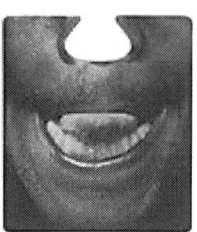

Preparation: get hold of some Face Mats (available for about £3 on Amazon) or print out pictures of some random faces and cut off the top halves. Make copies of the Your Character sheet. The children will also need a set of mirrors to look at their changed faces.

1. Unsettle the children by not doing a warm-up exercise for once, but coming in with your Face Mat/photo mask on.

Say: [your name] isn't here today so I'm taking you for the lesson instead. You'd better behave, kids. My name's Baxter Davies, and I'm 45 and I'm a truck driver from Bolton. I used to be married, tied the knot when I was just 18, but my wife ran away after six months to join the circus. The last time I saw her, she was twenty metres in the air above me, swinging on the trapeze in a shiny gold leotard. She looked like a tropical bird. I couldn't watch as she somersaulted between the bars; it was too upsetting. I had to come away. No idea what happened to her after that.

Now I live on my own with my collection of pet tarantulas. They like it warm in the flat, and so do I. If I'm feeling generous, I let them out of their tanks for a little explore. They enjoy climbing up the curtains, then dropping back down onto my head. Cute little guys. Hairy, though. You wouldn't want one crawling down the back of your shirt.

The worst thing that ever happened to me was when I had to try and save a drowning boy. I spotted him messing about on the side of the metal bridge as my lorry drove past. He was balancing on the railing and showing off to his mates. Idiot.

Straight after, I had to pull up the cab because of road works, but I carried on watching the boy in my rear-view mirror. Next thing I knew, he'd disappeared from sight. There was only one place he could have gone: downwards. I turned off the engine, threw open the door, leapt out and ran to the railings. There he was,

Boost Creative Writing Confidence at KS2 by Kate Long

splashing about in the river below, a circle of white foam with a dark dot on the middle. The other boys were yelling at me to do something. They were out of their minds with panic. So I had no choice, it was jump in or just stand and watch him go under.

The water was like liquid ice. I tell you, I've never felt anything so pure-cold, I thought my lungs would collapse. But I caught my breath, then started swimming towards him. His eyes were rolling in his head, he was that frightened. When I reached him, he grabbed onto me and started to force me under. He wasn't thinking. I had to act fast, peel his fingers away from my arm, get round behind him and hold him under the chin so I could tow him to the bank. He was coughing and flailing and choking; it was horrible to hear. My body felt like it was made of lead. Honestly, I can't tell you how we made it to the shore. When I felt the shore under my feet I could have wept with relief. I hauled him onto the mud and he was sick, right there next to me. With his hair plastered to his face and his white skin he reminded me of a little ghost. But he wasn't dead. He was alive. And that was down to me. I'd saved him. I was a hero that day. Just for that day. Because, to be truthful, I'm not normally what you'd call the hero type.

I wouldn't like to do it again, though.

2. Take off the mask, come out of character and ask what the children thought of Baxter. Is he a good man or a bad man? How much do we know about him? Would you like him as a friend? Was he really a hero? Conclude with the idea that people are complex and a mixture of good parts and bad parts.

3. Give the children their own masks/Face Mats. Let them have a giggle for a minute, then give out the Your Character sheet.

4. Ask if anyone's getting a sense of who their new character is? Hear any ideas.

5. Ask them to fill out the sheet with as much information as they can manage.

6. Share.

7. The children could obviously develop this anecdote into something longer.

Your character:

Name?

Age?

Job?

Married?

Children?

Personality type?

What's the most exciting thing that ever happened to them? Write your answer below.

Boost Creative Writing Confidence at KS2 by Kate Long

Boost Creative Writing Confidence at KS2 by Kate Long

26. Disappearing Whales (poetry)

Preparation: bookmark the YouTube videos **Orca Killer Whales Chasing** and **Huge whales swimming and jumping close to boat,** or any other video clips showing whales moving in the water. The first of these videos has haunting whale song in it, so turn the volume up when you play that one. The second is good because it shows the sheer size of the whales in relation to humans.

1. Warm-up exercise could be something to do with words relating to size.

2. Show clips from the videos, then ask the children for their impressions. Ask what they know about whales. Introduce some useful terms such as 'pod' for a group of whales, 'calf' for a baby whale, 'blowhole', and 'breaching' (when whales jump out of the water). Explain that whales are mammals, that they are the loudest animals in the world and that once, millions of years ago, whales lived on land and walked but they evolved to live in the sea. Share synonyms for 'largeness' and also for the sounds whales make, and put these up on the board.

3. Then read out the following prompts and ask the children to write a few words or a phrase in response to each prompt. As usual, stress that if anyone gets stuck on a particular line, they should just miss it out. You may want to suggest an opening for the last line: "If one day there were no whales left…"

4. Share and give feedback. We sent our poems on to the Japanese Embassy to ask if their new laws on whaling could be reviewed. The children really liked that idea. So far we have not heard back, but the poet Brian Moses has published our work on his blog, **brian-moses.blogspot.com**.

Boost Creative Writing Confidence at KS2 by Kate Long

Swiftly swoop through the water
echoing crying voice
water explodes excitedly and beatifuly from the whale.
fascinated fishes Whales are the Ruler of the Ocean
Dashing by corals red boats drifting by shining
lights of a colorful light house and others whales
injured

Silent oceans sad slow
no more exitment just a lonley blue wide sea
keep whales

Y5 work

Boost Creative Writing Confidence at KS2 by Kate Long

🐚 How you imagine their personalities...

🐚 How they have evolved over millions of years...

🐚 The sheer SIZE of them...

🐚 How they move through the water...

🐚 The sounds of the ocean as a pod of whales move through it...

🐚 What it looks like when a whale uses its blowhole...

🐚 How the other creatures of the sea might regard the whales as they pass by...

🐚 Some things the whales have seen on their travels...

And how you feel about the idea of there one day being no more whales left...

27. On Another Planet (description)

Preparation: snaffle some paint chart strips from your local DIY store, or Google 'pantone' and print out some similar swatches. One for each student is ideal, but one between two will do. You might also want to play them a very short clip of the film Avatar; at the moment there's a lovely 3-minute video available on The Literacy Shed website at **literacyshed.com/the-sci---fi-shed.html**, or just Google The Literacy Shed and once on the site, search for Pandora.

1. For your warm-up exercise, use a prompt about space or planets or stars.

2. Give out the colour chart strips. Ask the children what colour they've got. The likely answers will be basic — red, green, grey etc. Now ask them to lay the strip down on some paper, and write next to each colour the most accurate description they can come up with. Do one together so they get the idea: palest grey, dove grey, cloudy sky, steel, thunderstorm grey. Remind them they can use comparisons with nature and the world around them. If any complete this short activity super-early, they could swap with another student and try a different colour.

   When they've finished, ask a few children to hold up their strips and report back to the class what colours they found.

Boost Creative Writing Confidence at KS2 by Kate Long

3. Brainstorm on the board what words the class know for red (e.g. scarlet, crimson, ruby, blood red, tomato), for blue (aqua, sapphire, navy, sky blue, baby blue), for green (lime, olive, emerald, fir, grass green), for yellow (butter yellow, sunshine yellow, lemon, cream). Explain how very precise colour description can bring a piece of writing alive.

4. Now the children are going to go a piece of individual guided writing. As usual, though, tell them that if they get stuck on a question, just to leave it move onto the next one. Set the scene: **you've been sent to explore an amazing new planet that's covered in jewels. These jewels have to be collected and brought back to earth. Reports so far of the planet are that it's full of stunning colours and fantastic life forms. You're going to write about what you see when the spaceship door opens.**

   - **The door opens and the first thing you see is the weird-coloured sky with strange clouds or stars or comets moving across it. Write a line describing it.**

   - **You climb out of the spaceship and stand on the planet's surface. It's like nothing you've ever seen before! Write a sentence describing what's under your feet.**

   - **Ahead of you is something like a wonderfully exotic tree or tall plant. Write a sentence describing the height, the leaves and the fruit or flowers.**

   - **Something astonishingly bright flutters or flies past you. Describe it.**

   - **You walk past a pool, but the liquid doesn't look like water. Write a sentence describing what it looks like.**

   - **Finish with a sentence explaining how you feel about being on this strange new planet.**

5. Share and enjoy feedback!

28. The Magic Ring (story-writing)

Preparation: if you can provide some cheap rings for the children to handle, that's great. But they could quickly fashion their own out of pipe cleaners or silver foil or ribbon, or you could use Haribo 'Friendship Ring' sweets.

1. Make the warm-up prompt something to do with magic.

2. Discussion: what would you do if you were invisible? Ask the children to make a list of advantages and disadvantages to being invisible. What would an evil person do with such a power? What would a trickster do?

3. Read them this story:

You're in a strange city, wandering around the shops, looking for a present for your mum. You go down an alleyway, off the busy main street, where it's quiet and the buildings look older and shabbier. A shop sign catches your eye: *Unique Jewellery*. So you peer into the grimy windows and you can just make out a tray of very cool rings with a sign saying "The best gift you'll EVER give".

You push open the door and enter the shop. Inside it's dim and cluttered, packed with amazing objects. In the corner towers a stuffed grizzly bear, balancing a spotted teapot on its paw. A live robin hops from perch to perch, eyeing you cheekily. There's a spiked German helmet from World War 1 dangling from the ceiling above your head, and a row of fairy lights shaped like cats' eyes are twined round the shop counter. The floor seems to be made up of pound coins set in plastic. Somewhere far off, a music box tinkles faintly. You try not to sneeze at all the dust.

Then the shopkeeper emerges from behind a red velvet curtain. He's small with a face like a monkey and bright, clever eyes. He asks you want you want and you say you'd like to take a closer look at the rings.

Without another word he steps forward, reaches into the window, brings out the tray and places it before you. Your eyes boggle. They're all amazing. Which to choose?

Boost Creative Writing Confidence at KS2 by Kate Long

The more you stare, the more one ring draws your attention. In fact, it's started to glow faintly. When you reach out to touch it, there's a little prickle of electricity and a blue spark. You catch your breath. This is the ring for you. You hardly dare ask how much it is.

But the shopkeeper has read your thoughts.

"For you, today, that ring only costs one penny," he says. "You and that ring are meant to be together."

Your heart's beating fast. 1p? He's got to be mad. Best to pay the guy and get out of the shop! Quickly you fumble in your pocket and draw a penny out. It looks ridiculous. Nevertheless, he snatches it in a cool, dry hand, and with his other passes you the ring. Before he lets it go, though, he whispers to you: "Use it wisely, or else."

And then, suddenly, you're out on the street again, with no memory of opening the door or walking through it, and when you turn and check behind you, the shop has vanished.

4. Give out the rings, or whatever they're making rings out of. They can fashion their own ring and wear it while they write.

5. Now tell the children: this ring, that you knew was magic somehow, turns out to make you invisible! And you're going to tell the story of what happened next. Looking back at your list of advantages and disadvantages, explain how you used the ring and what happened as a result. Is this a happy story or a tale of disaster?

6. Share and give feedback.

Boost Creative Writing Confidence at KS2 by Kate Long

29. Spoon Wars (playscript)

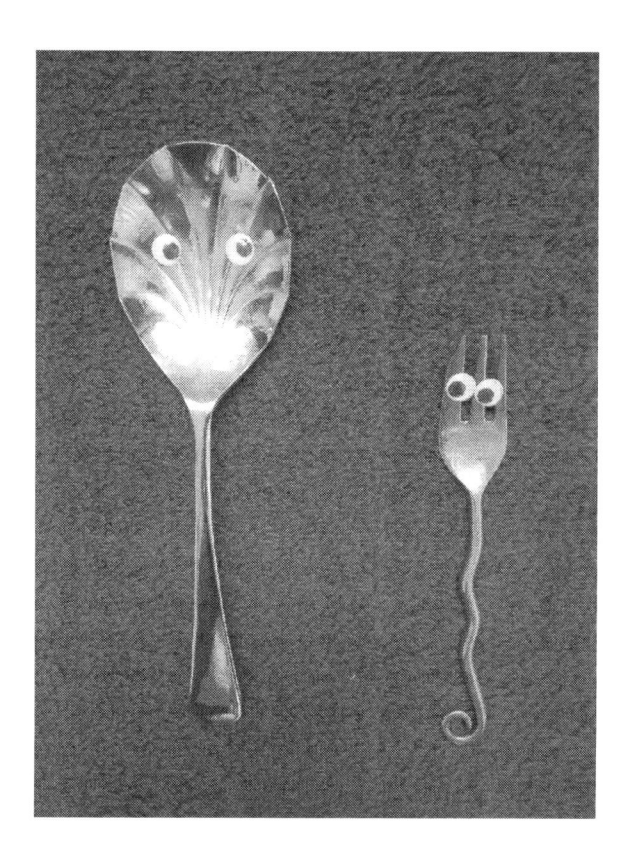

Preparation: get hold of some stick-on googly eyes. Assemble enough spoons/ forks/ safe kitchen implements for the children to have roughly two each. (You may need fewer if you want them to work in pairs.)

Stick eyes on a fork of your own, ready to use as a character.

1. Warm-up exercise.

2. Say to the children -

Do you ever stop to think what happens when your house is empty? When you go off to school, and your parents go to work or out to the shops, and the place is silent? Have you ever thought it might not be?

What if the things you use every day have a life of their own?

Boost Creative Writing Confidence at KS2 by Kate Long

What if the chair you sit in thinks, "Ooof!" when you sit down? Or the wellie you carelessly splash through a puddle thinks, "Eugh, now I'm all wet!" Maybe the taps think, "Not so tight!" when you turn them off. Maybe the blunt crayon in the pot is silently screaming, "Sharpen me!"

And how do they all get on, these things that live in your house? Does the big joint of meat in the fridge bully the little yoghurt pot? When you close the drawer on your socks, do they all start to fight with each other? Do your school shoes complain that your trainers pong? Does the nice clean soap in the bathroom shout insults at the toilet roll?

I've brought someone along today who'd like you to think about the kind of life she has, and she's brought some friends along with her.

Hold up your fork so the children can see it has eyes, and look at it expectantly. Bring it near to your ear as if listening to it.

Forky, is there anything you'd like to tell us?

Assume the voice of the fork.

I don't suppose you've ever stopped to think what my life is like. Shoved head-first into boiling hot food, and then – eugh – stuffed into your gaping mouth and sucked clean. Then after the meal, thrown into the dishwasher or sink and bombarded with detergent. After THAT tossed into a drawer with the knives and spoons, and the spoons are SO snooty, and the knives are SO aggressive. Horrible. It's even worse if you get into the wrong compartment. Once I spent whole night with knives. I was lucky to survive. Mind you, some of the other forks aren't very nice...

Lower the fork, frowning, and resume speaking in your own voice.

That's enough from Forky. She's getting hysterical.

Now I'll give give out some of Forky's friends, and some stick-on eyes, and you're going to write a short playscript of a conversation between two pieces of cutlery. You can work in pairs, threes or on your own. Be ready to read it out/perform it later on...

☆

Notes: although this is a light lesson built for fun, it revises playscript format which in turn could be a lead-in to paragraphing direct speech.

Boost Creative Writing Confidence at KS2 by Kate Long

30. Shells (poetry)

Preparation: assemble some shells, ideally enough so the children have one each. They needn't be fancy shells, any ordinary UK sea shells will do.

Print out some A4 Colour Wheels by googling **Tombow Dual Brush Pen Color Selector** or **The Martian Colour Wheel**. Be lavish! It's worth the ink if you laminate them to use again and again, because honestly, this colour wheel is one of the most useful tools for creative writing I've come across. But you might want to strim off or amend any American spellings in the sheet's title.

Make photocopies of the 'My Shell' sheet below.

You could also provide magnifying glasses for a really thorough examination of the shells.

1. Warm-up exercise could be something to do with the sea.

2. Give out the shells and let the children inspect them for a minute or two. Then ask what they already know about shells. You could tell them:

Boost Creative Writing Confidence at KS2 by Kate Long

Shells are made from something similar to chalk, but harder. They are the armour for molluscs (what is a mollusc? Oyster, snail, clam, mussel etc). Shells protect the animal inside and they give it its shape instead of bones inside the body. Different shell shapes serve different purposes: lots of frills, ridges and spines are there as protection. Smooth shapes help the animal to escape quickly and burrow down into sand. Some of our most familiar fossils are of mollusc shells. (Ammonites.) One of the oldest shell collections was found in Pompeii. Very big shells for sale have often been taken while the animal was still alive, and then the animal's been killed, so try to avoid buying large, fancy shells from shops. Picking up little shells from the beach is fine.

3. Ask the children -
   How do the shells feel under your fingers? (Temperature, texture? Invite similes.)

   What patterns can you see? (Similes?)

   What colours can you see? Use the Colour Wheel to list them.

   What shape is your shell? (Similes?)

4. Then ask them to fill in the 'My Shell' sheet. Stress you are not looking for complete sentences because this is poetry. A single word or short phrase might be enough for some lines.

5. Share and praise.

My Shell

How does the shell feel under your fingers?
_____

What patterns can you see?
_____

List all the colours on your shell:

Complete the sentence:

Fragile as _____

Describe the shape. Does it remind you of anything?
_____

List three things your shell has seen while it was living under the sea.
_____
_____
_____

Where did your shell end up when it was washed ashore?
_____

Boost Creative Writing Confidence at KS2 by Kate Long

31. Werewolves! (persuasive writing)

Preparation: make photocopies of the speech template on the next page. Write the character roles on slips and fold up tightly, or put into envelopes if you want the added drama. Every child needs to have a slip. You can give the slips out at random, but you might want to choose who gets to do the howling at the end.

For extra fun, you can write the slips on rice paper using an edible-ink pen then the children can eat the evidence and keep their secret extra-safe!

Remind the children before they start the werewolf bit not to get too gory in their ideas. These are fun werewolves, not scary ones.

1. Warm up prompt could be "The howling came from the forest".

2. Say: **terrible news — over Christmas, three of you were bitten by a werewolf. This means, at least one night of the month, you turn into a ravenous, out-of-control animal who doesn't even recognise the people you love most. You're safe during the day, but the full moon will trigger you to turn. Worryingly, even a tiny scratch from a werewolf will infect another person forever, and there is NO CURE. So what we need to do today is have a debate about what we do now. Do we get rid of the werewolves among us (and if so, how?) or do we try and keep them with us in the community?**

   - **I am going to give you slips with your character on it. Keep yours out of view, and DON'T spoil it by trying to look at anyone else's. Three of you will be werewolves but you'll also be something else as your ordinary daytime job. Look at the slip I'm going to give you, and if there's a little W after your job title, that means you're a werewolf.**

(Give out the slips, together with a template sheet for everyone.)

Boost Creative Writing Confidence at KS2 by Kate Long

- **Now you'll have ten minutes to write a speech to try and persuade everyone here of your point of view.**

(Hold up the speech template sheet)

- **You start, "Ladies and gentlemen…"**
- **Then you say who you are, and state your view** *("I think the werewolves should stay in the community", or "I think the werewolves need to be sent away")*
- **Give reasons for your view**
- **Explain what practical action you would take to deal with the werewolves**
- **Close the speech by stating your view again**

When we've heard the speeches, we'll discuss as a group, then vote about what to do. THEN we'll try to guess who in the room is a werewolf. Finally, those three people will reveal themselves by standing up and giving a howl.

Follow-up: this exercise has proved so popular, I've re-run it with vampires and zombies as the issue, just changing the wording.

Boost Creative Writing Confidence at KS2 by Kate Long

"Ladies and gentlemen:"

(say who you are and state your view)

Give a reason for your view: -

Give another reason for your view:

Give another reason for your view:

Explain any practical action you'll take to make your plan work:

Close the speech by clearly stating your view again:

Boost Creative Writing Confidence at KS2 by Kate Long

Character roles for the werewolf exercise

doctor   primary school teacher   secondary school teacher <u>w</u>

nursery teacher   chemist   butcher   supermarket manager

schoolchild aged 6   schoolchild aged 16   bus driver

vicar   café owner <u>w</u>   farmer   farm worker

retired person aged 79   nurse   police officer

local mayor <u>w</u>   security guard   headteacher

gardener   ambulance driver   PE teacher

school secretary   firefighter   pilot

hairdresser   pet shop owner   car mechanic

circus entertainer   artist   film-maker

Boost Creative Writing Confidence at KS2 by Kate Long

32. Horror Scopes (comedy writing)

Preparation: check a page of horoscopes in the newspaper. Ensure they're suitable to read out.

Make copies of the copyright-free zodiac signs sheet.

This exercise needs to be done on A3 paper and the children will also need scissors and glue.

1. Ask if anyone knows what a horoscope is? Root 'horo' = *hour, time*. 'Scope' = view. So a horoscope is basically the ability to see all the hours including the ones in the future.

2. Where do you come across horoscopes? What sort of things do they say? Explain to the children that because they are made up, they are incredibly vague, e.g.:

- *You'll get great results if you put in the effort.*
- *It's a good day to call someone you haven't seen for a while and ask how they are.*
- *Don't worry too much about small things.*
- *If you don't understand something someone says, don't be afraid to ask for an explanation.*

3. Ask when children's birthdays are, explain about Star Signs, and read some horoscopes out first from the genuine one in the paper and then from the silly version in this book.

4. What would happen if horoscopes were really specific?
- Today you'll meet a woman with red hair who'll hit you over the head with a wet fish.
- Tomorrow you'll win £4, 512 on the lottery.
- On Wednesday, as you walk home, a runaway piano will squash your foot.

Boost Creative Writing Confidence at KS2 by Kate Long

Tell the children they're going to making "Horror-scopes" — fun versions with silly and hugely unlikely advice. Show them how to divide the A3 sheet into 12, and give out the zodiac signs so they can cut them out and stick them on before writing underneath them.

5. When the task is finished, have fun reading each other's whacky horoscopes!

Capricorn ♑ 22 Dec - 20 Jan	Aquarius ♒ 21 Jan -19 Feb	Pisces ♓ 20 Feb - 20 Mar	Aries ♈ 21 Mar- 19 Apr
Taurus ♉ 20 Apr - 20 May	Gemini ♊ 21 May - 21 Jun	Cancer ♋ 22 Jun - 23 Jul	Leo ♌ 24 Jul - 23 Aug
Virgo ♍ 24 Aug - 22 Sept	Libra ♎ 23 Sept - 22 Oct	Scorpio ♏ 23 Oct - 22 Nov	Sagittarius ♐ 23 Nov - 20 Dec

Gemini (May 21 – June 20): You'll discover an identical twin.

Cancer (June 21 – July 22): Beware of statues falling on top of you.

Libra (September 23 – October 22): Remember to dye your hair blue today!

Scorpio (October 23 – November 21): Avoid cucumbers.

Aquarius (January 20 – February 18): If someone offers you a Polo mint, say no.

Pisces (February 19 – March 20): You'll meet a man with a banana on his head. Avoid!

Aries (March 21 - April 19): You will find a hamster inside your swimming kit.

Taurus (April 20 - May 20): Alligator steaks for tea!

Leo (July 23 - August 22): Try to speak German all day — it's good luck!

Virgo (August 23 - September 22): Don't trust anyone who has tentacles for fingers.

Sagittarius (November 22 - December 21): If you have a pet cat, re-name it Billy Bignose.

Capricorn (December 22 - January 19): Someone will try to steal your soap — be vigilant!

33. Lifetime Achievement Award (comedy writing)

Preparation: You'll need a willing accomplice to play the part of the award winner. A pupil will do, but it's funnier if you can persuade another adult to step in. (The speech is written about a female character, so if you choose a man or boy you'll have to adapt the pronouns and perhaps a few details.)

Having a little cup or shield to hand over is a nice touch; borrow one from the school trophy cabinet. Finally, make a copy of the speech below to read out to the class.

Prime the children to raise enthusiastic applause, whooping etc. when you've finished talking, then introduce your 'winner'.

1. Warm-up exercise.

2. Ask your accomplice to stand up, then read out the following speech.

   We're here today to present a Lifetime Achievement Award to someone very special: _____, scientific prize-winner and Olympic champion, and widely regarded as one of the finest Bond villains ever.

Boost Creative Writing Confidence at KS2 by Kate Long

At just 14 she showed she was headed for stardom when she won BBC Young Musician of the Year with a version of Rachmaninov's Piano Concerto which left all four judges weeping with emotion. Two years later she accepted a place at Lincoln College, Oxford, to study nuclear physics, and whilst there she won the Marie Curie prize for discovering how to stop bacon rashers from sticking to the frying pan.

Having completed her degree in less than six months – and gaining First Class Honours – she moved to Spain where she began to ski professionally, conquering every black slope in the Pyrenees and then quickly being selected for the British Olympic team. She won four gold medals for her country before a cruel injury – she tripped over her husband's slippers – forced her to give up a brilliant sporting career.

[Shropshire] called her home, but not for long. A text from a casting agent meant she was soon back on our TV screens, this time in the hilarious comedy 'That's Not My Dog', a cult show which won three BAFTAS and a Golden Rose at the Montreux comedy festival. A sell-out tour followed, where _____'s fans packed theatre after theatre to watch her unique stand-up comedy style. Even a teenage Prince Harry confessed he sneaked along one night to see the show.

As her thirties approached, she gained the role that was to make her a household name: Madame Arachnid, the villain James Bond falls in love with. Indeed, her performance in 'The Man with the Golden Leg' was so inspired that the director immediately wrote her into the next Bond film, 'Die Fall'. Sales of merchandise from both were brisk, and a Madame Arachnid figurine can now fetch as much as $600.

_____ took time out to raise a family and teach at _____ school where she was much-loved, but in the evenings she returned to her scientific roots, working on a cure for that thing where your glasses mist up when you open an oven door. Millions of people are now free to peer in at their Sunday roast without going temporarily blind, thanks to her. With her earnings she set up the _____ Foundation to promote free skiing lessons for UK children.

Recently she has become known as the new Voice of the X Factor, and also as the author of the hilarious teen fiction series 'Gilbert Baboon'. Her books

Boost Creative Writing Confidence at KS2 by Kate Long

have topped the bestseller charts now for three years, and the cartoon version of 'Gilbert Baboon' on CITV is its most popular show ever.

So tonight, _____, we honour you with this Lifetime Achievement Award, and say thank you for everything you've contributed to the world. Please step forward and take your cup.

(Cue wild applause.)

3. Explain to the children that they are going to imagine themselves in the future, then write their own speeches, either about themselves or a friend. They need to imagine the kind of glories they'd like to achieve in life and then go as fantastical as they like. Brainstorm some arenas in which they might excel and list them on the board, e.g.

   TV/theatre/film
   books
   sports
   charity
   science/medicine
   music/art/dance
   cookery
   adventure/endurance/bravery

   The students in my writing club found it helpful to divide their page up into decades: My 20s, My 30s, My 40s etc.

4. At the end of the session, the children who want to can deliver their speeches while the others clap as if they were at a real awards ceremony.

34. Tiny, Rubbish Superpowers (comedy writing)

Preparation: get hold of something that will do as a cape – a square of bright material is fine – and maybe cut out a black a cardboard mask. But the cape is the main thing.

1. Warm-up exercise.

2. Tell the children to make a list of superheroes/villains they know, and their superpowers. Share.

    Discuss which would be the best superpower to have!

1. Tell the children you have to leave them for a moment. Walk out of the room and put on the cape/mask. Fling the door open and stride back in. Announce you are a superhero and your amazing powers are:

    - you can look at ANY tree and immediately know how many leaves are on it.

    - you can turn milk chocolate into dark, and back again.

    - you can make any cat come up to you for a stroke.

    - you can recite your 117 times table.

    How useful are those powers? Can the children imagine any situation where one of those powers might save the day?

3. Ask the children to write the heading TINY, RUBBISH SUPERPOWERS. Tell them their task is to come up with as many really useless superpowers as they can. Then write a short description of how those powers failed to be any use at all in an emergency situation, e.g. a collapsing bridge, an erupting volcano, and escaping villain.

4. When everyone's got at least three powers written down, the children can come up to the front and perform the same dramatic entrance you did, using the cape/mask. Then the class can vote for the most rubbish superpower.

Boost Creative Writing Confidence at KS2 by Kate Long

5. If the children want to extend the activity, they can write a whole story featuring their rubbish superhero and the disastrous situations she/he gets into.

35. Gotcha! (playscript)

Preparation: If the children are not sure about how to set out a playscript, photocopy a sample page or put one up on the projector so you can talk through the layout.

1. Warm-up exercise.

2. Tell the children they will be writing a dialogue, and if they don't know the term, explain that a dialogue is two people talking to each other.

3. Check everyone understands how to lay out a playscript.

4. Put the children into pairs. If anyone's left over, they can partner you. One person will be A and the other B.

5. Ask A to write the opening line: **"I know what you were up to last night."** Tell them they are going to write the rest of the dialogue together, but before they start they must spend two minutes thinking about some questions. You can write these on the board.

   Who are A and B? What is their relationship with each other?
   (Talk through possibilities – are they friends, enemies, rivals, a bully and a victim, a policeman and suspect, a parent and child?)
   Where is the conversation taking place?
   What was B up to?
   What is B's reaction to being found out?
   What is A hoping will happen now?
   Who comes out on top?
   When you're sure they've addressed at least the first three questions, let them start.

6. At the end of the writing session, the children can perform their dialogues and get feedback.

Boost Creative Writing Confidence at KS2 by Kate Long

36. A Rap (poetry)

Preparation: Google 'instrumental rap beat' and find one you like the sound of.

There's currently a nice clip on YouTube called *Hip Hop Beat Boom Bap Rap Instrumental Sad Piano – Prod. By Ben Maker* by 90s Old School Rap Beats, where the graphic is just a still of a piano keyboard and a rose, nothing violent. The beat is fairly slow, too, which will make it easier for the children to speak along to it. But search around till you find something you like, and bookmark it.

You will also want an example of a kid-friendly rap you can play them to get them in the mood. I like this YouTube one about vegetables: *Vegetable Rap! Song for kids* by YTKidsVids.

If you're feeling really inspired, write a rap verse about yourself ready to read to them. Mine is truly awful but it doesn't matter: the children like it a lot when I join in, and that makes them happier about reading their own rap out. So if you can, screw up your dignity and have a go.

My name is Mrs Long and I like to write

I'm a peaceful type, never pick a fight

I have two guinea pigs and one crazy hamster

Every Wednesday evening I'm a Zumba dancer

I work at Criftins, which is really cool

It's my absolute, number one, favourite school.

OK, that's enough of that!

1. Warm-up exercise.

2. Ask the children if they know what a couplet is. Break down the word, so couple = 2 (it's not "cup-let"). Begin a few orally, and see if they can finish them:

Boost Creative Writing Confidence at KS2 by Kate Long

- **Humpty Dumpty sat on a wall...**
- **Twinkle twinkle little star...**
- **An apple a day...**
   What is the rhyme pattern here?

3. Write some beginnings of couplets on the board and see if the children can finish them. Suggestions in brackets in case everyone's mind goes blank!

   - **Hello there, tiny bumblebee...** *(I really hope you don't sting me.)*
   - **My silly dad trod on the cat...** *(It had been sleeping on the mat.)*
   - **I climbed into my racing car...** *(I drove it fast, I drove it far.)*
   - **My sister lost our new football...** *(She kicked it over next door's wall.)*

4. Tell the children they are going to write a rap using rhyming couplets, and that the subject of the rap will be themselves. They could include things they like or don't like, information about their family, pets, school, or sport clubs. If you're feeling brave, read them your own.

5. Play them a little bit of a child-friendly rap so they get an ear for the rhyme and rhythm.

6. Let them write at least 4-8 lines, and explain they'll be reading those lines out over a rap beat. That might be the time to perform your own, if you can bear it.

7. Share/perform. If you can record them speaking, the children love listening back to their raps.

37. Line Breaks (poetry)

Preparation: make photocopies of the Poetry Lines and Bird Table worksheets on the next pages. Have scissors, coloured paper and glue available for the children to use.

1. Warm-up exercise.

2. Give out the Poetry Lines sheet and talk it through. Stress there are a lot fewer rules in poetry-writing than in ordinary writing (prose), so we have to rely on instinct and feel our way much more when we're writing a poem.

3. Give out the Bird Table sheet and explain to the children how they are going to cut up the lines and lay them out to make a poem. Where they begin one line and end another is entirely up to them. But they should be looking at how words at the end of a line can have extra power, and so can very short lines. Stress there is no right and wrong here; it's just about what feels right.

4. Give them a quick flash of what the finished product will look like (see next page).

5. When the exercise is finished, let the children compare notes with each other. Are there any particular lines that work well?

6. It would be good to follow this session up with some poetry-writing of the children's own, then they can practise playing about with line length and line breaks.

Boost Creative Writing Confidence at KS2 by Kate Long

Poetry Lines

When we write a rhyming poem, it's clear where we need to end a line.

*Tyger! Tyger! burning **bright**,*
*In the forests of the **night**,*
*What immortal hand or **eye***
*Could frame thy fearful symme**try**?*

But when we write non-rhyming poetry - Free Verse – we have to rely on what "feels right".

Compare:

I watched an eagle spread its wings wide against the sun.

A kestrel hang, then swoop.

A robin hop hop across the frozen grass.

I watched an eagle spread its wings wide

against the sun.

A kestrel hang,

then swoop.

A robin

hop

hop

across the frozen grass.

What is the effect of breaking the lines up? Does placing certain words at the very end of lines make them feel any different?

Boost Creative Writing Confidence at KS2 by Kate Long

Bird Table

Dawn breaks. In the first light, a robin hops up, picks seed, darts away. Next are the jackdaws, large and fierce with their stabbing beaks. Their black wings flap like Dracula's cape. They strut, they squabble, then take off as one angry cloud. Here comes a wren now, tiny as a mouse. It jerks and bobs between the leaves, and vanishes. Two fat pigeons land clumsily. Up and down the grass they stump on straw-thin legs. They blink, confused. Their heads tilt. Suddenly there's a whirr of feathers and the hawk descends. Everything scatters before her yellow claws. Beady-eyed she swoops, searching for prey. But the garden is quiet as a graveyard. She circles lazily, glides up once more, and moves on. No birds here.

Boost Creative Writing Confidence at KS2 by Kate Long

Bird Table

Dawn breaks.
In the first light, a robin hops up,
picks seed,
darts away.
Next are the jackdaws, large and fierce with their stabbing beaks.
Their black wings flap like Dracula's cape.
They strut, they squabble,
then take off as one angry cloud.
Here comes a wren now, tiny as a mouse.
It jerks
and bobs
between
the leaves,
and vanishes.
Two fat pigeons land
clumsily.
Up and down the grass they stump on straw-thin legs.
They blink, confused.
Their heads tilt.

Suddenly there's a whirr of feathers and the hawk descends.
                                      Everything scatters
before her yellow claws.
Beady-eyed she swoops, searching
for prey.
But the garden is quiet as a graveyard.
She circles   lazily,
glides up once more, and moves on.

No birds here.

Boost Creative Writing Confidence at KS2 by Kate Long

38. Mushrooms (poetry)

Preparation: buy a cheap pack of mushrooms, ideally enough for one between two students. (They're currently on sale at Lidl for 90p per pack of about 20.) Choose ones where you can see the gills underneath, so not button mushrooms.

1. The warm-up exercise could be something to do with fungus or mushrooms.

2. Give out the mushrooms and let the children have a good look at them. However, do NOT let them handle roughly, as mushrooms are not robust and will fall apart if battered or picked at. If necessary, joke that you want them back for your tea! Stress also that these are shop-bought mushrooms, and the children must never ever fiddle with fungus they find outdoors as it might be deadly poisonous.

Ask them what they know about mushrooms – where they grow, what the pattern underneath the cap is called *(gills)*, how they spread *(spores, not seeds)*. Other interesting facts: mushrooms are not plants or animals, they belong to a separate group of their own. They have their own immune system that helps fight off disease, and they can make their own vitamin D in sunshine like we can. Some fungus glows in the dark, and in ancient times people carried it through the forest like torches.

3. Tell the children they are going to describe a mushroom as if to someone who's never seen one before. Get them ready to respond to these prompts in writing, but as usual remind them that if they can't think of anything, just leave that question and wait for the next one.

- **What shape is the top of your mushroom? Does it remind you of anything?**
- **What colour is it? Be precise.**
- **What colour are the gills underneath?**
- **What pattern do they make? How are they arranged? Does it remind you of anything?**
- **What does the stalk feel like?**

Boost Creative Writing Confidence at KS2 by Kate Long

- **Sniff the mushroom. What does it smell of?**
- **When mushrooms stand in a field, how much noise do they make?**
- **What do they remind you of as they stick up out of the grass or soil?**
- **Think of a single adjective that sums them up.**

4. Share and give feedback.

39. Crows (editing)

This is quite a demanding task and more suited to Y6.

Preparation: make copies of the crow poems on the next page and cut them into 2.

Make copies of the tabby cat sheet.

Find an image of a crow to put up on the screen.

1. Warm-up exercise could be something to do with birds.

2. Discussion: what is poetry? See if the children can come up with a definition. Ask: if you look at a page, how can you tell whether the writing there is poetry or prose? Does poetry have to rhyme? Does it have to have a regular beat? What was the first poetry you ever heard? *(nursery rhyme?)* Does anyone know any poetry off by heart? *(If some students are saying they don't, ask if they know some song or hymn lyrics. Make the point that this is poetry too.)* What do we use poetry FOR?

3. Explain that above everything else, poetry is a stripped-down form of writing. In poetry you can take out lots of the little words you have to use in prose and just leave the important ones. This can give the poem more of a punch.

4. Give out the Tabby Cat sheet and read it through. Ask the children whether the poem gives the reader as much information as the piece of prose.

5. Give out Poem A. Ask the children to work in pairs to see if they can cross out some of the words to make the poem better. This is quite a demanding task, so it might be an idea to pair up children of different abilities, then the ones who are less confident can have support. Also, before they start, do a couple of examples on the board together.

Boost Creative Writing Confidence at KS2 by Kate Long

Example 1: **The boiling hot mouth of the volcano glowed red and crimson and a whole lot of smoke was pouring out of the top of it.**

could be trimmed to:

The boiling mouth of the volcano glowed crimson. Smoke was pouring out.

(You don't need 'hot' if you have 'boiling'. You don't need 'red' if you have 'crimson'. You don't need 'of the top of it' because where else would the smoke be coming from?)

Example 2: **The friendly dog bounded forward eagerly, full of happiness, wagging its tail and trying to lick us.**

could be trimmed to:

The dog bounded forward eagerly, wagging its tail and trying to lick us.

(You don't need 'friendly' or 'full of happiness' if the dog is wagging its tail and trying to lick.)

6. After the children have had a chance to cut some of poem A, give out Poem B and ask the children to compare the two. Why is B more powerful? Go through the poem line by line and talk about why some words can go.

7. In a follow-up, the children could write their own animal poems, having studied online a galloping horse, a running dog, a leaping cat etc. But they should be paring the words right down so only the important ones remain.

Tabby Cat

My cat is a tabby. She moves gracefully, padding lightly on her feet and swishing her tail. Her eyes are green and her tongue is pink and rough when she licks your hand. She can jump onto the fence from a standing start, and balance there. It's as if she's not really tame at all. She's more like a wild animal. (61 words)

Tabby cat

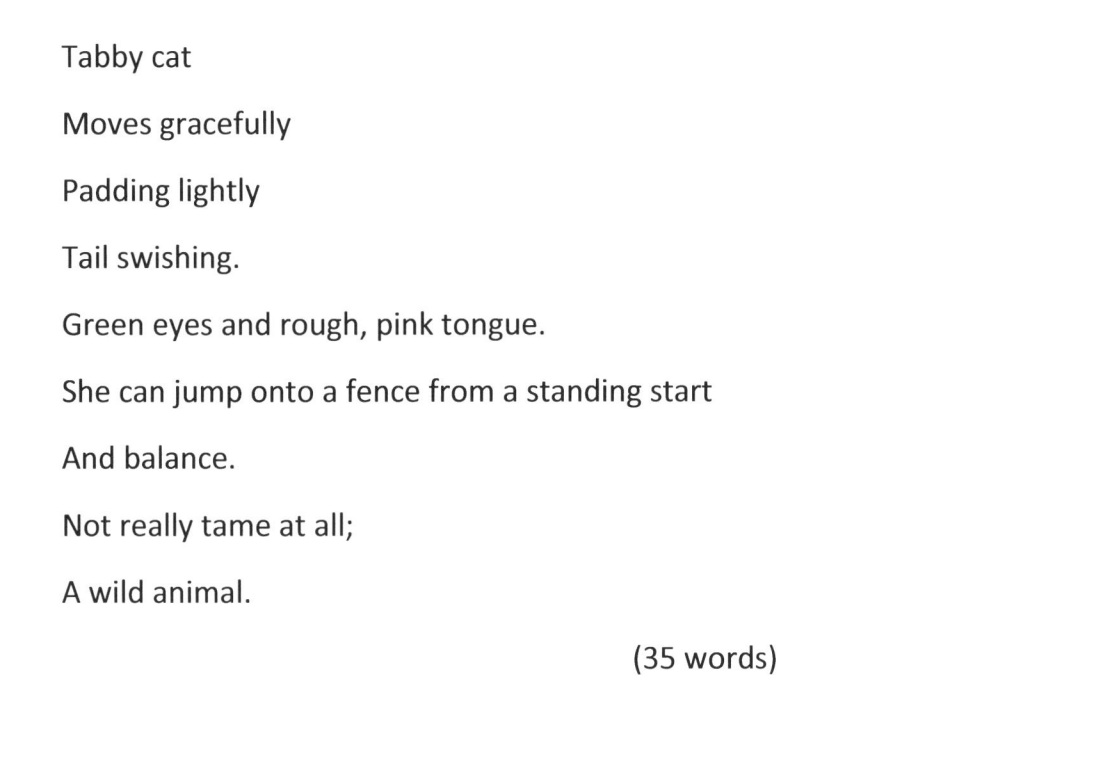

Moves gracefully

Padding lightly

Tail swishing.

Green eyes and rough, pink tongue.

She can jump onto a fence from a standing start

And balance.

Not really tame at all;

A wild animal.

(35 words)

Does the poem tell you as much information as the first piece of writing (prose)?

Boost Creative Writing Confidence at KS2 by Kate Long

Poem A

The crow's beak is a lot like a very pointed dagger

The crow's feet end in curved claws that are sharp

Its wings are like glossy black fans

Its eyes are like bright beads

Watching you all the time.

It has a proud and noble expression

The crow stands about like a soldier on duty

Then, when it takes off it flaps its wings, rises up into the sky

And rides the air currents like a surfer

Poem B

Beak like a dagger

Feet which end in curved, sharp claws

Wings are glossy black fans

The eyes bright beads

Watching.

Proud and noble

The crow stands like a soldier on duty

Then takes off

Rises

Rides the air currents like a surfer

40. Dandelions (poetry)

One for summer!

Preparation: collect a few dandelions so the children can have some on every table. Find images or short YouTube clips of dandelion clocks. Or, if you are brave, try bringing some dandelion clocks into the classroom — or running the lesson outside.

Make photocopies of the examples of elfje poems on the next page. Assemble some magnifying glasses.

1. Warm-up exercise.

2. Check everyone knows what a syllable is. Clap names. Clap long words. Clap monosyllables.

3. Explain the term **elfje** = Dutch for 'little eleven'. Elfje poems are poems consisting of eleven syllables spread over five lines. The structure goes:

    1
    2
    3
    4
    1

4. Look at the sheet of examples. You could do one together on the board, too.

5. Give out dandelions. Play the video clip of a dandelion clock opening.

6. Let the children write their own elfje poem about either the dandelion flower or the dandelion clock. If anyone finishes, they swap and can do other one. If anyone races through those while the rest of the class is still working, tell them to write an elfje poem about an animal, or about a person they know.

Boost Creative Writing Confidence at KS2 by Kate Long

Hamster

Fat,

furry,

warm, orange.

Sits in my hand:

snug.

Dog

Keen

tongue pants,

tail wagging,

bright eyes watch me.

Friend.

Fish

Quick!

Silver!

Flash of steel!

Underwater

ghost.

Boost Creative Writing Confidence at KS2 by Kate Long

Examples just for you, the teacher:

Dandelion

Bright

gold coin.

Fallen sun.

Feeds the friendly

Bee.

Dandelion Clock

Sphere.

Fragile.

Tells the time.

Round-headed cloud

- Gone!

Writing Activities 3

(a bit of a faff, but worth it)

41. Precious Jewels (poetry)

Preparation: Assemble some plastic jewels; I got mine for pence from the craft section at Home Bargains, but many supermarkets and pound shops sell them. They've proved a terrific investment because I've been able to use them for so many different writing activities. They feel quite special and the children love them. But if you can't find any, just print out some picture of jewels. Ideally every child should have a jewel/picture of their own. If you've gone for pictures, then leave out prompt question 2, or ask the children to imagine.

1. The warm up exercise should tap into the idea of jewels – 'jewel' or 'gem' could be your prompt word, or 'treasure', or 'buried treasure'.

2. Give every child a jewel and let them handle it, hold it up to the light, try and count how many facets it has. Make sure they know the names that go with the colours, e.g. that red is a ruby, and write up on the board the spellings of 'emerald', 'sapphire' and 'diamond' (and 'amethyst' if you have any purple ones).

3. Explain how jewels are formed — *(same way as rocks and fossils, underground, millions of years ago, through process often of tremendous heat and pressure).*

4. Ask the children what we use jewels for, and why. *(Incredibly rare, incredibly tough and long-lasting, incredibly beautiful.)* Mention kings and queens, burial chambers and pyramids, rings with magic powers, e.g. The Philosopher's Stone, pirates, thieves, swords with jewelled hilts and crowns, any dramatic stories they might have read featuring jewels. They might know some computer games with jewels in them, e.g. Spyro and Pokémon, but try to keep the conversation steered towards the mystical/historical.

Boost Creative Writing Confidence at KS2 by Kate Long

5. Discuss: how many colours/shades can they see in their gem? Make a helpful checklist of words on the board for each colour, such as scarlet, crimson, blood, tomato, rose, sunset; aqua, turquoise, ice, navy, sky, bluebell, sea-blue; moss, lime, cat's eye, olive, fir tree, grass. Can anyone add to these lists? Where in nature do you see colours like that?

6. Now they are ready to write. Deliver these prompts at whatever pace suits the group, and remind them that if they get stuck on one, just to wait for the next line.

   - **List all the colours you can see in your jewel. Be as precise as you can.**
   - **How does your jewel feel to touch? (Touch any pointed corners as well as the flat sides.)**
   - **Describe the shape, using a simile if you can. (Hint: think about things in nature that are small, hard, rounded.)**
   - **Where has your jewel been lying before it was discovered?**
   - **Remember, your jewel was formed a long, long time ago. List three historical events your jewel might have seen during its life.**

7. **Go back and think of a title for your poem.**

8. Share the poems and give feedback.

A Special Gem

Lime, fluorescent, neon and teal
Emerald leafy, all shiny and sparkly
Smooth like a pebble but sharp as a spear
Don't blink twice for it might disappear.

Just the size of a baby bird's beak.

Hidden inside the deepest cave, surrounded by
An underwater lagoon
Filled with colourful wildlife.

This gem has seen the darkness fade and the sunlight grow,
The wars wage and the peace break
The tip of a stalagmite drop and a stalactite rise
But most of all our evolution and soon
Our extinction.

Y5 work

42. I Am (personal writing)

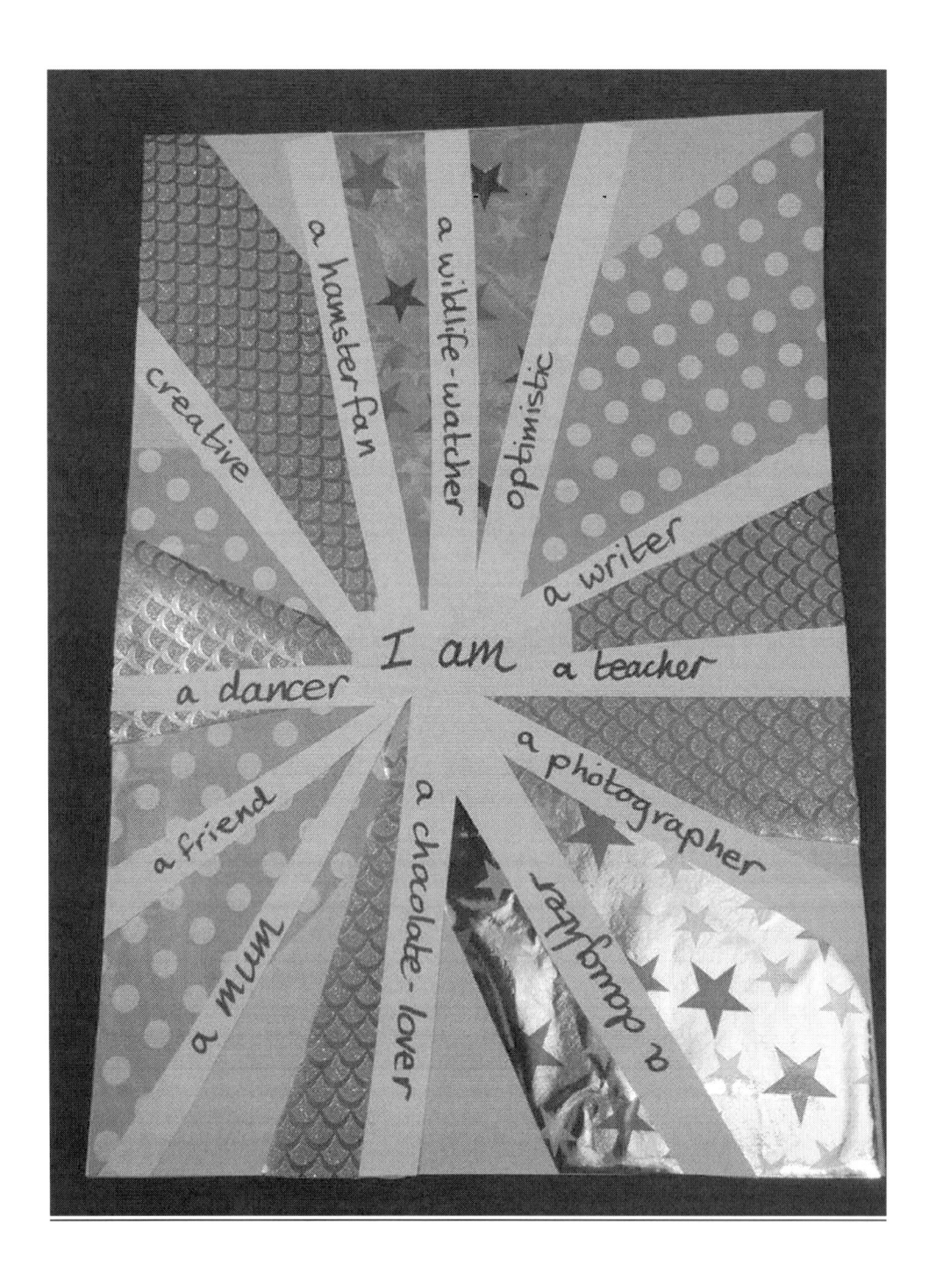

Preparation: print this image (there is a colour version on **schoolwritingclub.blogspot.com** entitled 'I Am' and dated 6th November 2018). Alternatively, make up an 'I am' poster of your own. Then assemble glue, scissors, A3 paper or thin card, plain white paper and some off-cuts of wrapping paper. Pages from old magazines could also be used for the background patterns.

Boost Creative Writing Confidence at KS2 by Kate Long

1. Warm-up activity.

2. Get the children to brainstorm all the things they are in different contexts/to different people. For example, who are they in a family sense? A son? A sister? A nephew? A granddaughter? Then ask them to think about all the skills they practise in school and what that makes them - a writer, a mathematician, a footballer, a gymnast, an artist, a cartographer, a scientist, a linguist etc. The next section should be about their personalities: are they curious? Calm? Energetic? Thoughtful? Hilarious? Finally ask for anything that hasn't been covered - nationality and heritage, for example. Stress the information should either be neutral/factual, or positive, nothing negative. Also, they mustn't put anything down that they're not comfortable sharing.

3. When they have their lists complete, ask them to consider what amazing individuals they are! (As I said to them, 'We all have bad days when we make mistakes and think we're rubbish. Stick this poster on your bedroom wall to remind yourself that you're absolutely not.')

4. Next, show them the 'I Am...' sheet and explain they are going to make one of their own. After that, the students really need very little direction, as long as they can see the example to use as a template. My own group took two sessions to complete the task, one for preparation and one to put the poster together.

The 'I Am...' poster would make a nice start-of-term/ getting-to-know-you lesson for any class. As well as a writing club activity, this could also be something you could do in a Learning Mentor session to help build up a child's self-esteem.

In terms of grammar, it's a good exercise in turning verbs and gerunds into common nouns ("I am...well, I like playing the piano...so that makes me...a *pianist*").

43. Bubbles (poetry)

<u>Preparation</u>: get hold of some bubble pots – Tesco currently do a pack of 6 for £1.50. Or make your own bubble water with detergent and give the children straws to blow bubbles with.

However, one commercial bubble pot between two or even three or four children would work fine, as long as they are sensible about taking turns, because one person can blow while the others observe.

Make copies of the Bubble worksheet on the next page.

1. Warm-up exercise could be:
- 30 seconds to list things that are incredibly thin
- 30 seconds to list things that are incredibly fragile
- 30 seconds to list things that are incredibly quiet
- 30 seconds to list things that are transparent
- 30 seconds to list things that are stealthy/ sneaky
- 30 seconds to list anything that disappears

2. Give out the bubble pots. Depending on the group, you might have to be strict about spills; maybe bribe the children with some free bubble-blowing time outside afterwards if they're good.

3. Ask them to blow a bubble carefully and then hold it up to the light. What can they see? Shapes, patterns, colours? What's the skin of the bubble like? Is it still, or does it move? What happens at the moment the bubble bursts? Allow the children to do this several times. If they're working in pairs or more, one could blow and the others focus on watching. When you feel they've had enough time to observe, stop them and put the bubble pots to one side.

4. Give out the bubble worksheets and ask them to fill in as many lines as they can. As usual, if they get stuck on any of the lines, they should just leave that one out and go onto the next.

5. Feedback and sharing.

Boost Creative Writing Confidence at KS2 by Kate Long

Bubble

Thin as _____

Bulges like _____

Trembles like _____

Floats away like _____

Round as _____

Fragile as _____

Across the surface _____

Quiet as _____

Disappears like _____

Looking at Bubbles

Thin as diamond shards
Bulges like a toad's neck
Trembles like an earthquake
Floats away like the leaves in autumn
Round as the red sunset on a summer's eve
Across the surface is a spider's web full of multicolour flies
Quiet as a snake slithering towards its prey
Disappears like your night-time dream.

Y5 work

44. Peacock Feathers (poetry)

Preparation: get hold of some peacock feathers, ideally enough for at least one feather between two children – you can currently buy 10 for 89p on eBay.

Google "Martian colour wheel" and you'll end up at the site of Warren Mars who has designed one of the most useful tools I've ever used for creative writing. It looks like this, except in colour:

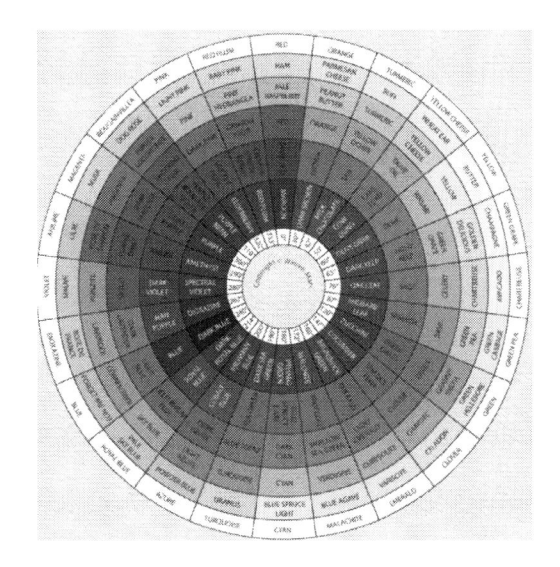

It not only shows a stunning range of shades, it names them too, instantly giving children the vocabulary they need to describe what's going on with the feather. I've printed out a set on photographic paper for the children to use over and over again. A real boon to teachers of creative writing! Another great colour wheel can be found by googling **Tombow Dual Brush Pen Color Selector**, though you may want to strim off the American spelling in the title.

Finally, make photocopies of the peacock feather worksheet on the next page.

1. Warm-up exercise.

2. Give out peacock feathers. While the children are examining them, tell the story of Argos, 100-eyed giant and servant of Hera, queen of the gods. He was set to guard Zeus, her husband, but fell asleep at his post and was killed by Hermes who bashed him on the head with a rock. Hera was so upset, she

took Argos's hundred eyes and put them into the tail of the peacock. And that is why peacocks have such glorious tails.
3. Give a very quick lesson on the parts of feathers – the shaft is the rigid spine that runs up the centre, the vane is the flat part, and the barbs and barbels are the individual strands of the feather which can be pulled apart gently and then 'zipped back up' again.

4. Give out the colour wheels. Ask the children to write down as many colours as they can match.

5. Compare notes.

6. Give out the worksheets and ask the children to fill in as much as they can. Ask them to avoid 'an eye' for question 3, unless they specify what sort of eye it is.

7. Sharing and feedback. These notes can now be written up as poems.

If you can't get your hands on any peacock feathers, this lesson could be adapted to work with other types of feather.

My Peacock Feather

Waves around like_____

Soft to touch as_____

The pattern reminds me of_____

List all the colours you can see_____
_____

The barbs and barbels are like_____

What was your feather designed for?
_____

Peacock Feather

Waves like shimmering wheat in the golden fields
Soft to touch as the fresh fur of a new-born bear cub
Cyan, clover, light azure, delphinium blue, olive oil, cane toad
Each barb is like a lone tree in the aftermath of a forest fire
This single feather was hand-picked to keep the ancient goddess
in the summer months cool.

Y5 work

45. Snails (poetry)

Preparation: gather some snails, two or three per table. After rain is a good time to find them. They especially like to cluster under the overhang of a wall. Keep them beforehand in a lidded container with air holes in the top, line the bottom with something damp and absorbent, e.g. moss, and give them lettuce to eat. Kept cool and dark they should be fine for 48 hours. In the classroom, it's best to decant the snails into bug pots as they can move more swiftly than you'd think! Gather magnifying glasses so the children can observe closely. Afterwards, return the snails to the spot where you found them.

Make photocopies of the Snail Questions sheet.

1. Warm-up exercise could be something a bit different to get the children thinking along snaily lines.
    - 30 seconds to write down things that move slowly.
    - 30 seconds to write down things that revolve.
    - 30 seconds to write down things that are squishy.
    - 30 seconds to write down things that are small and round.

2. Hand out the snails. Stress the importance of being kind to our visitors. Let the children have a really good look.

3. Ask what the children know about snails. Give them some snail facts: **they are gastropods, one of earliest animal types to evolve; they can be found on land or water; they belong to the same family as the octopus; they have no bones. There are 60K species of snail. They use muscular waves on their foot to move, and the slime they ooze cuts down friction. They can't hear but they can smell and see. They are mostly nocturnal. Each snail is both male and female. Life expectancy can be as long as seven years. The shell is made of calcium carbonate, i.e. chalk. Most snails are vegetarian. They have rows and rows of tiny teeth that scrape against the food to grind it away.** Ask the children to observe their snail very closely. What's on the end of its tentacles?

Boost Creative Writing Confidence at KS2 by Kate Long

What does its mouth look like? How is it moving? What's the pattern on its shell?

4. Tell the children you are going to give them sheets which they can use to write a poem about their snail. For once you'd prefer it if they <u>didn't</u> answer in complete sentences – notes are better for making poetry.

5. Let them make notes, and then draw the class together for a discussion on what they've seen.

6. Collect in the snails and give the children some quiet time to turn their notes into a poem.

Snail Notes

1. (Size – what is it as small as?)

2. (Colour and pattern on shell?)

3. (Shape of shell?)

4. (Colour of flesh?)

5. (Texture of flesh?)

6. (What are the horns doing? Do they remind you of anything?)

7. (What's happening underneath the snail?)

8. (Does it remind you of any other animal?)

9. (Pace – just HOW slow is it?)

Boost Creative Writing Confidence at KS2 by Kate Long

<u>My Snail</u>

Size of a 50p coin.

The shell is like frozen waves of different shades of brown

A circular spiral.

The flesh is the colour of pondwater.

The horns are searching for something

They remind me of a blind man's cane.

Underneath, waves of mucus are travelling through the body.

Sloth

Slow as a spider making a web.

Y5 work

46. Gothic Tales (story-writing)

Preparation: make copies of the gothic image sheet on the next page. These images are all copyright-free.

Practise making mini books out of a single sheet of paper. There's an excellent Youtube video called *Easy Mini Notebook from ONE sheet of Paper — NO GLUE — Mini Paper Book DIY — Easy Paper Craft*s by Red Ted Art, but there are instructions all over the internet on how to make these little books.

Make one yourself and stick in some pictures to show the effect you're after.

1. Warm-up exercise should be something like 'midnight' or 'darkness'.

2. Discussion: what do we mean by the term "Gothic"? There are modern Goths, who wear black, but in literature it means a particular style of story or poem. The most famous Gothic story is probably 'Frankenstein' by Mary Shelley, written in 1818. Does anyone know what it's about?

Boost Creative Writing Confidence at KS2 by Kate Long

The main elements of Gothic writing are spookiness and mystery, so things like *(write these on the board)* locked rooms/boxes, towers/castles/ruins, dreams/omens, bats/wolves/ravens, red and black, night/moonlight, storms. There's a sense of mystery/danger/threat.

3. Show miniature book, explaining that they are going to start a Gothic story of their own. To illustrate it, they can either stick in the pictures from a sheet you'll give them, or they can draw their own.

4. Here's the directed writing exercise. As usual, go at whatever pace suits the group, and stress that if anyone can't think of an answer to a prompt, they should just miss it out and wait for the next.

    - **It's night-time, with a full, brilliant moon. You're somewhere in the lonely countryside, standing in front of some huge, imposing iron gates. Describe what you can see around you.**
    - **What sounds can you hear?**
    - **Write a sentence about how you pushed your way through the gates, and how you were feeling.**
    - **Describe the path you start to walk down.**
    - **You pass a statue: describe it. (Use plenty of detail.)**
    - **A bird is watching you from a branch overhead. Describe it, and say how it made you feel.**
    - **You're approaching an old, half-ruined mansion. Describe the state it's in what it looks like.**
    - **As you get near to the door, you spot an interesting-looking key lying on the ground. Write a sentence about this moment, and how you pick up the key.**
    - **Suddenly a strange figure runs out and stands in front of you. What does she/he look like?**
    - **The figure speaks to you. What does he/she say?**

5. Share and give feedback. Obviously this story can be carried on and finished. Then, in a follow-up lesson, you'd get the children to make their books and copy the story into neat, with illustrations.

Boost Creative Writing Confidence at KS2 by Kate Long

Gothic images to cut out and use

Boost Creative Writing Confidence at KS2 by Kate Long

47. The Invasion (story-writing)

Preparation: gather enough coloured pipe cleaners so every child can have one. Thicker ones are best. You'll also need to hole-punch some black paper so you have lots of little black circles, or white ones which the children can colour in with a black pupil, like the picture below. Have glue available in the classroom.

Make your own furry worm, ready to show.

Make photocopies of the Furry Worms prompt sheet.

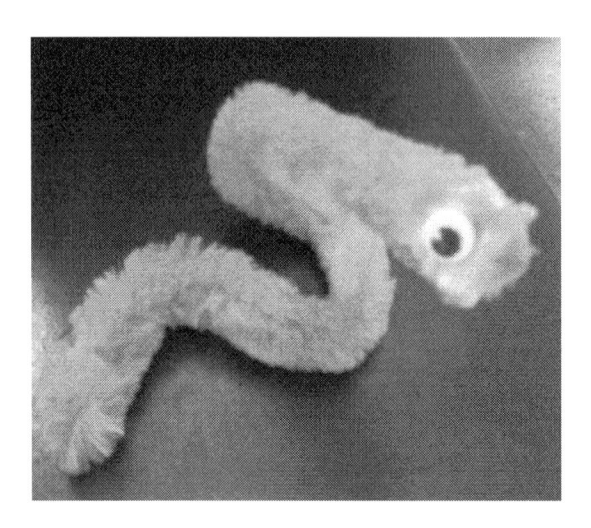

1. Warm-up exercise. Maybe something to do with aliens?

2. While waving your own furry worm about, tell the children this story: **at the end of the summer holidays, builders had to come in and mend the pipes underneath the school buildings. They had to dig deep down, and while they were digging, they uncovered a small cave and a network of tunnels leading off it. When they shone their torches down the tunnels, these creatures are what they saw! Never before known to science, and without names, the furry worm-things swarmed to the surface and as soon as the children were back at school, they began popping up all over the place and causing BIG problems! You are going to explain what happened next...**

Boost Creative Writing Confidence at KS2 by Kate Long

3. Give out the pipe cleaners and let the children make their own furry worms by sticking paper 'eyes' onto one end.

4. Ask them to put their worms into the following poses: sleepy – alarmed – threatening – sneaky.

5. Give out the prompt sheets and give the children a few minutes to jot down notes.

6. Then it's time to write the story.

7. Sharing and feedback.

Furry Worms

What are these creatures called?

How many are there?

How dangerous are they?

What do they eat?

What eats them?

Whereabouts in school do they like to make their nests?

They have an unusual power: what is it?

They cause the headteacher a big problem: how?

Someone in school turns out to be superb at handling them. Who?

Report back. Now tell us the story of one day when the worm-things created havoc, and how the children and teachers coped.

Boost Creative Writing Confidence at KS2 by Kate Long

48. The Magic Door (poetry)

Preparation: on thin card, make copies of the copyright-free door image. It's nice to have some stick-on jewels to decorate this, or some glitter pens or metallic gel pens. Home Bargains and many of the pound shops do them very cheaply. During the copying-up stage you'll also need sheets of A4 card, glue and scissors in the classroom.

Make your own 'opening door' before the lesson to show them how the work will be presented. Like the front opening door section, the back is thin card too.

Make copies of the '7 things that lie behind the magic door' sheet.

1. The warm-up exercise could be "Behind the door…"

2. Ask the children to imagine a portal, a door, that could open into another world. Say that lots of famous writers have used that idea. Have they read any books where that happens? To be able to enter another world is something that's fascinated people for centuries. Stories which use a magic door include *The Lion, the Witch and the Wardrobe, The Magician's Nephew, Alice in*

Boost Creative Writing Confidence at KS2 by Kate Long

Wonderland, Star Trek, Transformers, Monsters Inc, He-Man and the Masters of the Universe, Northern Lights, Super Mario 64, Minecraft, Miss Peregrine's Home for Peculiar Children.

3. Show them the door you made and talk about how they can decorate it when the writing's done. Or you can do the decoration first, and then write the poem. I actually did it that way round because it gave the children chance to think, and made them want to do their best writing to go inside the decorated frame.

4. Give out the sheet '7 things that lie behind the door'. You might like to talk some of the prompts through first, or alternatively, let them dive straight in.

5. Share and give feedback.

6. When it comes to copying up, we found it worked best when the poem was written onto a piece of narrow paper and that was stuck into the doorway, rather than writing directly onto the card. That way, if something went wrong and the poem ended up looking a mess, the pupil got to have another go without spoiling the frame.

7 things that lie behind the magic door:

Something incredibly rare and precious:
1._____
_____

Something fabulously dangerous:
2._____
_____

Something made of ice:
3._____
_____

Something made of fire:
4._____
_____

Something huge, vast, towering:
5._____
_____

Something that crawled out of a cave:
6._____
_____

Something that would take your breath away:
7._____
_____

Boost Creative Writing Confidence at KS2 by Kate Long

Magic Door

Behind the magic door
Is an enchanted charm from kings and queens
A curse of immortality you did not want
An ice shadow in the shape of a crown
A god statue, gold and on fire
Mount Everest
Elephants dancing on the moon in pink tutus.

Y4 work

49. Woodlice (poetry)

Preparation: first catch your woodlice! They're easy to find: just lift up a plant pot or log and collect as many as you need. Then pop them in a tub with air holes in the top. As long as they're kept cool and in the dark, with moistened paper towel and some decaying wood to eat, they'll be fine for up to forty-eight hours. Afterwards the woodlice should be returned to where they came from.

You'll also need magnifying glasses and bug pots. Before the lesson, decant individual woodlice into their pots. One woodlouse between two children is ideal, but you can probably work with fewer. (It might also be worth having a photo of a woodlouse printed out just in case a child claims to be too scared to be near a live one, although this has never happened to me and I've taught this exercise many times.)

1. Warm-up exercise. Maybe something relating to minibeasts?

2. Tell the children they will be writing about woodlice, and give out the pots. Remind them to be kind! Remind them how big they must look to the woodlice. Ask them what they know about woodlice already. Are woodlice harmful? *(No.)* Are they insects? *(No.)*

3. Give them some facts about woodlice:

    - they're invertebrates; they're related to lobsters; there are 40 different species in the UK including pink ones called Rosy Woodlice; they have 14 legs; their outer skin splits into two parts when they need to moult; they don't wee, they just release a gas; their blood is blue; they can live up to four years. They eat rotting wood and leaves. They like cool, dark, damp places eg underneath plant pots and logs. Baby woodlice hang onto their mum's underside as she scurries about. Predators include spiders, centipedes, toads and shrews.

4. Ask the children to examine the woodlice closely, using the magnifying glasses. Does the shape of the woodlouse's body remind the children of anything? See how the creatures move, especially the ripple effect of their legs. How are their bodies made up? Mention the word **segmented**, and draw the children's attention to the **antennae**. If anyone wants to know, the prongy

bits at their tail end are called **uropods** and they're there to discourage predators. What does the underside of the woodlouse look like?

5. Tell the children they are going to write some lines about their woodlouse, so they'll need to put the pots down and get their heads into the writing zone.

    Then dictate these prompts, at whatever speed is right for the group:

    - Write a line describing the shape of your woodlouse.
    - Write a line describing the precise colours of the skin.
    - A line describing how it moves.
    - A line describing some small detail, e.g. its antennae, legs, segmentation.
    - A line which is made up of one, two or three adjectives.
    - A line describing where it lives.
    - A line containing a metaphor or simile.
    - A line in which you imagine the woodlouse's personality.

Remind them that if they're completely stuck on a prompt, just leave it blank and wait for the next one.

6. Share.

7. Finally — get the children to wash their hands if they've handled the woodlice directly!

Boost Creative Writing Confidence at KS2 by Kate Long

Woodlouse

Like an armoured truck

Thunder grey and flecked with white

It is a heavy umbrella

It trundles and crawls, twitches and scuttles

The great brown monument of a tree is rough and intertwines with heaven

The long, pink neighbour worm, soft-skinned friend, hunts for food

Woodlice are dopey, acrobatic vampires.

Y6 work

50. Conkers (poetry)

One for autumn!

Preparation: collect some fresh conkers, preferably still inside their cases but ready to split open.

Make copies of the conker worksheet on the next page.

1. The warm-up exercise could be 20 seconds each time to think of:
   - something the size of your fist
   - something that is bright green
   - something that is spherical
   - something sharp or pointed
   - something very smooth

2. Share ideas from the warm-up exercise.

3. Give out conkers (with the warning that the spikes are sharp). Ask the children: where do conkers come from? What is a conker? Why are they spiny? Split them open. Examine conkers. Ask: what colours can you see? What are the markings on the surface like? What is it like to touch? Tell the children to go back and look at the casing, then stroke the inside. Ask: what colour is it? What does it feel like?

No one has ever before seen your conker. You are the first! What other things in life do you break open/unwrap?

4. Give out the conker sheets and ask the children to fill in as many lines as they can.

5. Sharing and feedback.

6. The best lines can be copied up to make a poem.

Boost Creative Writing Confidence at KS2 by Kate Long

The outside of my conker is:

(colour)_____

(shape)_____

(spines)_____

Opening my conker is like:

_____

Inside my conker is:

(colours)_____

(markings)_____

(to touch)_____

The conker sits inside its case

like_____

_____

My Conker

Pale green beach ball

Spines are sharp lead

Inside, my conker is the brown of a male deer

Markings like a mussel shell

Like glass to touch

The conker sits inside its case like an egg in a nest.

Y4 work

A last word

Running a School Writing Club

I believe there is a real appetite amongst most children to write freely, experimentally and for pure pleasure. Holding a regular writing club can provide that opportunity.

Because there's no formal assessment attached to the writing done in club – unless you count feedback from peers – that removes a great deal of the pressure some children associate with writing. There's also space here to pursue individual interests, and to enjoy spending time on presentation and artwork.

Here are some Writing Club 'rules' I've found work well:

- We always start the session with a warm-up writing exercise (see the first section of the book for examples).
- No child ever has to share what they've written if they don't want to.
- If someone does share work, feedback should be positive. Writing Club is a nurturing, encouraging environment.
- When others are reading out their work, everyone needs to be completely quiet and listen respectfully.
- Spelling and punctuation isn't something to worry about during this special writing time. What matters in Writing Club is getting words down, and exploring language, ideas and effects. However, it's very important that handwriting is legible!

If the club is an after-school one, a drink and a small snack is helpful at the start.

Giving the children a cardboard wallet or folder in which to keep their club work makes them feel like proper writers whose work is worth saving.

Regular in-house competitions for small prizes like notebooks, rubbers and novelty pens have proved popular. External competitions can also be flagged up and Writing Club time used to discuss or begin entries.

A termly display and/or an anthology goes down well as it shows the children how much you value what they've done. The self-publishing website **lulu.com** is easy to use if you want to create an attractive, professional-looking but reasonably-priced book. Incidentally, if I'm typing work up I consider it entirely fair to correct SPAG errors on the children's behalf, given that professional authors have copy editors to sort these things out for them!

Boost Creative Writing Confidence at KS2 by Kate Long

Boost Creative Writing Confidence at KS2 by Kate Long

A little early feedback...

Oh Kate, your book was amazing today! My Y5 English class came back from a sporting activity 30 minutes early and I had no idea what to do with them. I reached for your book and we did the warm up activity word association game. They then tried to put as many of their final words(which I'd written on the board) into funny sentences. They LOVED it!

It's the new year, so we wrote resolutions for aliens, sharks and bank managers, before pinching **Kate Long**'s excellent idea and writing Horror Scopes. My favourite is Aries: 'Try not to use the toilet this month'. Then we we wrote on strips of paper (and shuffled them) to make poems to be submitted to Spark Young Writers Magazine, so we did. So I h... See more

Boost Creative Writing Confidence at KS2 by Kate Long

You can see more creative writing ideas at my blog,
https://schoolwritingclub.blogspot.com/

Boost Creative Writing Confidence at KS2 by Kate Long

Printed in Great
Britain
by Amazon